BECOMING AN ECO-CITIZEN

EDWARD TITLES

ACKNOWLEDGMENTS

Dan Mitchelmore for his superb contributions, Carl-Johan Löwenberg for the excellent feedback Kathleen and Jannika for being a valuable set of eyes, the helpful eco-warriors, and as always Christian and Rasmus.

CONTENTS

INTRODUCTION

"What statement is more viable? To fit the finite world around our infinite wants or to tailor our wants to live within the constraints of a finite world?" – David W. Orr

Most people today are well aware of climate change and its causes. They have already seen or experienced sweltering summers and resultant forest fires and droughts. The torrential rain, flooding, and mudslides from the extra evaporated water. And if weather changes like these haven't directly affected you, changes to land use and food supply eventually will. Climate change is leading to food and water shortages, price increases, and possibly most terrifying of all, rising seas that will swallow up cities and homes in a surprisingly wide variety of places worldwide.

Suppose you haven't seen any evidence of these extreme climatic changes yourself. In that case, you are part of the lucky few and perhaps unaware, as many are, that wars around the world are fought for access to resources such as water made unavailable due to climatic changes. And in cities such as the iconic Jakarta, where it can't stop the rising waters, Indonesia is now spending $34 billion to build a new capital.

Even if all the media and designated experts do not convince you on climate, what is undeniable and largely undisputed, is that humans are polluting the world and putting immense pressure on its resources. Harmful chemicals are tragically abundant in our water, air, and soil. We have topsoil depletion, which in turn produces much less nutritious food. Our oceans get trawled by massive fishing vessels that harvest faster than those ecosystems can recover.

As we shall see, our current model doesn't make sense whether you look at this from a compassionate angle or a purely economic one. We allow our companies to externalize their costs, leaving us to pick up the bill (strictly, this is the cost of increased cheap goods, but it is unfair as not everyone uses or benefits from them). Added to this, the monopolies that some companies have in some industries, particularly in financial and energy markets, mean that the price of everything is going up.

These issues are so enormous and complex that you may feel it's too late to do anything. And if it isn't, indeed, it has to be some big, swooping action from the world leaders, influential organizations, or big business to fix it. What could you possibly do to help stop this crisis? – after all, you're just one person among nearly eight billion people globally.

Unsurprisingly, many people feel powerless when they think about the environmental crisis we face. The sense of powerlessness creates complacency. We end up doing nothing – or, going to another extreme, we hope that our refusal to use straws and recycling bins will be enough and put the issue out of our minds entirely.

And, sure, reducing the usage of plastic straws might save some sea creatures today. However, if we don't do more, there may be no more sea creatures to keep in the first place just a few decades from now.

This is where *Becoming an Eco-citizen* comes in. In this book, I hope to invite you on a journey of sustainable living through adopting a lifestyle that will make a long-lasting impact on the planet, yourself, and your community. Becoming an Eco-citizen is not about personal greenwashing or the extremes of turning into a fully zero-waste, dumpster-diving, one-shower-a-week eco-warrior.

Instead, it's a road in the middle, a way of looking at the world through slightly different eyes and making small but impactful daily decisions. And if you become a boat canal-dwelling, zero-air-travel plant-based climate activist by the end of it, more power to you.

However, becoming an Eco-citizen is not about being radical – it's not about drastically upturning your entire life. For one, trying to become a model citizen for sustainable living overnight isn't sustainable. If you've ever gone on a diet or told yourself you'll get on a CrossFit every day, you'll know that most ambitious all-or-nothing attempts tend to crash and burn within the first week. On the other hand, if you take it step-by-step and consistently make minor changes, your chances of success increase dramatically. It's the same with becoming an Eco-citizen: instead of trying to take on too much, too fast, this book will guide you towards more consistent steps you can take every single day that will eventually form a lean, green, and healthy lifestyle.

In addition, I hope to clarify some confusion surrounding most green choices. You're one day convinced that soy milk is best at one point, only to find out soy is almost as bad as dairy the next day. Or you may think electric cars are the solution, then read a study on the negative impacts of lithium mining or that coal power stations are what's powering that car. Your vegan lipstick may contain harmful toxins, and your biodegradable detergent may be depriving rivers and streams of oxygen – the list goes on and on, and with so much contradicting information out there, making meaningful choices can feel overwhelming. *Becoming an Eco Citizen* will help you navigate this and make informed decisions.

This book focuses on a sustainable lifestyle and mindset rather than a list of "green-approved" products or quick tips on composting your biowaste (there, of course, will be some of that). And sustainable means not only living in a way that follows what the Earth can provide but is also doable for an extended, sustained period. Just like one month of the gym in January, one month of 'Veganuary' isn't going to cut it (and sends all the wrong demand signals to companies producing vegan products). This is why it's counterproductive to expect sustainable living in an unsustainable way. We need more people doing better, not a few doing best. Becoming a vegan, outfitting a whole house with solar panels, and buying all green products are not viable for many of the population or those who have just not bought into living in line with the planet's resources. However, this does not mean they can't be doing a few things better and should be encouraged and not disheartened when an 'eco-martyr' criticizes their efforts.

As someone with a background in education, I'm passionate about helping people understand the issues we're facing and offering tools and techniques to embrace a sustainable lifestyle instead of throwing out yet another listicle of "10 Ways to Go Green". This book is not a list that will only offer a few simple solutions without making a more prolonged, lasting impact. Becoming an Eco-citizen is a journey, not a quick fix, but the further down the road you travel, the easier the path will become.

The stats are in. Eco-citizens are on the rise, and I invite you to find your way of sustainable living through this book.

PART 1

THE SELF

WHAT IS AN ECO-CITIZEN?

Eco-citizen (noun): An inhabitant of the world who is ecologically informed, understands the global economy and energy, and makes decisions based on what is feasible in today's highly complex world. An Eco-citizen has a toolkit they can use to make a difference – to themselves, those around them, and our precious natural resources and heritage.

The author Scott Fitzgerald is attributed to have once said that the sign of an intelligent person is being able to hold two conflicting ideas in their head simultaneously. As an Eco-citizen, you will have to do a lot of that. Sometimes the environmental impact is needed to enable human flourishing. Some things are bad for the environment but good for us, and both may be true. Being an Eco-citizen is a balancing act between the want for human flourishing and protecting our habitat.

NATURE IN AND OF ITSELF HAS NOT ALWAYS BEEN KIND to human livability. When we think of nature, we think of the beautiful sunsets, a rich ecosystem of plants and animals, or the majestic landscapes it produces, but there are always two sides to every story. Mother nature is cruel as well as kind. Until recently, most humans lived a hand-to-mouth existence and would be lucky to see 40. For most of history, the cold was much more of a menace to human survival than the heat. 98% of species were already extinct before we came along.

Far from being a pristine garden of Eden that we have come along and destroyed, the world is more like, as Alex Epstein put it, a 'wild potential' that has just as likely tried to kill and support us. It's sometimes difficult to see in this modern world we have created for ourselves, but it was a long, complex, and massive undertaking to manipulate the world to make it habitable for humans. Without even primitive clothing and shelter, most places in the world would not be fit for human habitation. Central heating, electricity, and air conditioning have helped us make the world fit for human life, and unfortunately, there isn't an action that doesn't impact the world somehow. As Eco-citizens, we weigh all the pros and cons and make balanced decisions based on improving the average person's life and protecting the beautiful and essential parts of nature.

Sphere of Influence, Sphere of Concern

In his infamous book, Seven Daily Habits of Effective People, Steven Convey talks about your sphere of concern and your sphere of influence. It's one of the many models in that that helps when making decisions. There are many concerning things going on around the world, and frankly, there is nothing most individuals can singly do about it. Eco-citizens focus on issues within their sphere of influence, things that they can directly affect, as opposed to highlighting the injustices in the world but not being able to do anything about it. If your sphere of concern is too much larger than your sphere of influence, you will start to feel like things are hopeless, and you will be much less effective as an Eco-citizen. This is why as Eco-citizens, we deal with the truth that some things are beyond our influence and look to do better in the things we can directly affect. This book will touch briefly on the big picture of our current environmental/energy needs, those issues that are more significant than we can influence. It is helpful to have a general overview, but ultimately, we want to be working on the things we can make a difference.

The Fossil Fuels Paradox

Let's start with some of the hard truths about our world. It would be easy to write a book saying things like "fossil fuels bad, solar and wind good," but unfortunately, in our complex world, nothing is that black and white. There are still around a billion people out there who live on less power than a refrigerator and have not even begun to fully harness the energy of fossil fuels, never mind thinking about green energy sources. Even with the developed world seemingly pushing to get rid of them, it is very likely that fossil fuel usage will only grow in the coming years as people use their unique benefits to pull themselves out of poverty. For these billion people, getting enough calories, clean water, and shelter are their primary concerns, and the abstract idea of climate change is minor.

With all the talk of greenhouse gases and their adverse side effects, it's easy to forget that fossil fuels, the machines they power, the abundance they have helped create, and the free time they have enabled have allowed people to think and innovate, which in turn has pulled the average person out of poverty. They are what allowed us to master our environment and build the modern world we live in today. In many cases, they eliminated the need for manual labor when humans created machines to do the job for them. Powered by fossil fuels and producing far more than 'human power', fossil fuels have lifted billions of people out of bondage. The 'unpowered' people of the world have this right, too. As much as fossil fuels contribute to climate change, nothing comes close to lifting people out of poverty more than a cheap, abundant, highly concentrated, easily transportable on-demand energy source. And for the genocidal types who believe fewer people are the 'solution' to our environmental woes, nothing reduces birth rates more than coming out of poverty.

For the rest of us in the 'developed' world, we have much more wealth and technology at our disposal and, therefore, more options. We've had our industrial revolution. If we care about lifting humans out of poverty, we must realize that fossil fuel usage will only rise over the following years in some parts of the world. As carbon emissions rise, we may even have to be open to 'unnatural' ways of dealing with this. This fact makes the job of an Eco-citizen in the developed world a little more complicated, and the so-called 'solutions' are merely trade-offs. It is an Eco-citizens job to understand these trade-offs and pick the best one.

There are simple things the developed nations could do to lead the way. While generally unpopular with many green activists due to their own environmental impact, the use of nuclear and hydropower (a trend that has reversed in recent years) are currently the only economically viable ways to meet our massive energy needs carbon-free. We all know nuclear has its waste even though it can produce up to a million times more energy than oil. And hydro, while being renewable and responding quickly to energy usage spikes, must dam up rivers and disrupt the area. But even solar and wind are not consequence-free (rare earth mining, digging up the space for the long transmission lines, etc.) and use fossil fuels as a backup to compensate for the intermittent nature of these energy sources.

Even if wind and solar replace fossil fuels for electricity generation, this only constitutes a fifth of all fossil fuel usage. We have around 100,000 ships on our oceans essential for transporting food and goods (and people) globally that are nearly all fossil fuel powered. And approximately 30,000 aircraft, again all fossil fuel-powered. Electric versions of these things are in the making, but like electric cars, it would be counterproductive to power these things using fossil-fueled power plants. It would make things worse and create more emissions by being much less efficient. So much energy is lost in the process of converting fossil fuels to electricity and then into movement as opposed to directly from an engine.

Solar and wind, as of now, can't produce industrial heat needed in the mining, manufacturing, and construction sectors. As the famous economist Thomas Sowell says, "there are no solutions, only trade-offs." If greenhouse gases are as damaging as we think, we need to consider the trades like nuclear waste or the damming of rivers. Unfortunately, we can't have our cake and eat it. We seem to live in a world that tells us that we can cater to humans' massive energy needs with zero impact. As much as we'd love this to be accurate, this is a fantasy we must dispel if we are to deal with our current problems. Questions when concerning energy are never simple, and we must be willing to keep in mind there are effects and consequences which we still haven't uncovered. The delicate balancing act of living in a way the planet's resources can provide and not having humans slip back into a life of poverty is tough.

I feel we live in a world where politicians and thought leaders give people easy solutions that sound like there are no negative consequences. Please think of the recent pandemic. Yes, lockdowns slowed the spread of the virus. But they also led to increases in depression, domestic violence, and suicide (and most likely countless other things we can't measure with statistics). No solutions, only trade-offs.

That's enough about the things we can't change. Let's move to the things we can. The focus of this book is to look purely through an environmental lens, evaluate your sphere of influence/concern, and give you the tools to do something constructive about it.

Can You Make a Difference?

Who will save us?

   Governments? Technology? Elon Musk?

I'm afraid it's time for us to become Eco-citizens and take responsibility. Most of the technological solutions are here. As Eco-citizens, it's our job to help these solutions become commercially viable. While it's understandable that you may feel entirely overwhelmed by these huge environmental issues, it is a mistake to think you and your everyday choices don't matter. Every single person matters and every single choice makes a difference. My first vivid experience of this was with Napster, the first peer-to-peer downloading service that allowed everyone to download music illegally for free. My teenage self made a lot of lunch money at school selling pirated CDs. But when a friend of mine confronted me, saying it was harming the music business, my reply was, "little old me, what could I do to the giant music industry." Unfortunately, there was more than just "little old me" doing it, and the millions of people who thought their actions wouldn't harm a massive industry were wrong. A whole sector almost went bust, and it took years for them to recover and eventually move to a less profitable streaming format. The industry has never been the same since. Now artists/record companies use expensive live shows to make up for the loss of earnings.

Millions of people making small decisions work both ways, for good as well as evil. Let's put this into perspective.

There are almost eight billion of us on this planet. How can you alone make a difference?

The famous Paris Accord states we must keep temperatures rising another 2°C. The most significant contributor to global warming is greenhouse gases (GHG) emitted by burning fossil fuels for heat, transportation, and electricity. An average US citizen emits 19 tonnes of GHG per year; in the UK, the number is smaller – around 10 tonnes annually – but it's still nowhere near the 0-2 number we need to stick to if we're to keep the temperatures from rising.

And that's where you come in: if you reduce your GHG emissions by half, you prevent hundreds of GHG tonnes from entering the atmosphere. If you get your loved ones, family members, or community onboard, multiply those numbers by two, three, or 20. Now, the impact begins to snowball; imagine these actions multiplied by all eight billion of us.

And this is just one small example. By reducing our environmental impact, we're already solving the climate crisis. If we make healthier and more efficient lifestyle choices, like adopting a more plant-based diet, it may reduce our carbon footprint from food by a whopping 75% - almost as much as cutting down on air travel. Voting green with your wallet may have a ripple effect on supply and demand: remember how organic, vegan, sustainable products were a complete novelty just 15 years ago, whereas now, they're in abundance? That's the impact of buying from companies and manufacturers that offer sustainable solutions – if we demand better, this will force the corporations to do better.

You can also make an impact by deciding to reuse rather than recycle, traveling locally instead of only jet-setting to far-flung exotic places, and choosing sustainable options for your home, work, and family environment. Everything counts, and it adds up quickly.

Along your journey to becoming an Eco-citizen, you may also discover alternative living, eco-communities, and climate activism – but for now, take the first small step and expect a few bumps on the road. If you feel overwhelmed by that, consider what would be better: 10% of the population being 100% sustainable or 100% being 20% more sustainable? The math is straightforward.

Becoming an Eco-citizen doesn't mean you need to take the whole world upon your shoulders. It means getting informed, discovering a way of sustainable living little by little, and making conscious choices every step of the way. It's a philosophy and a way of being as much as a lifestyle. *Becoming an Eco Citizen* will not give you cheat sheets and lists of recommended products. Instead, it will teach you to make your own informed choices and make decisions that matter. How far you're willing to go is up to you, but this book hopes to show you the way and support you on your journey.

The World Is Connected

An Eco-citizen understands that the environment has no heed of artificially created borders. We have to look at the world as a whole:

- China's pollution is just as much our fault as it is our problem.

- The plastic thrown out in Europe could end up in someone's food in Africa.
- Our fast-fashion habit is negatively impacting the environment in Asia.

We're all connected, and becoming an Eco-citizen is understanding that we each have an impact on this global-ized world.

And while our Earth is bountiful with resources, they are still finite, and we should make it our aim to live within those limits. This is key: instead of comparing ourselves to others at different stages of their journey, we should focus on the mindful, achievable steps we can do ourselves right here and now. There will always be someone out there doing better than you, but you can be an inspiration to someone who is just starting.

We have to be prepared to see the bigger picture and scratch deeper than the surface. Even this book has an envi-ronmental toll, so why damage the world and publish it? We need to look further than that (and hopefully, the combined efforts of the readers will offset the damage caused). This book is about developing an eco-centric way of looking at the world, and once you have that, you will be resourceful enough to start on your way of sustainable living. It's not easy: I can tell you that as I'm writing from my canal boat and the fire has gone out, it's January, it's cold, and I don't have the luxury of switching on the heating. But it's the life I chose, a decision based on my personal life experiences and other inputs that have affected my worldview, and for me, the payoffs outweigh the setbacks.

That doesn't mean you need to move into a tiny house

or a boat this minute, aim to be zero waste by the end of the week, or never buy a new item. It's not realistic, and this level of expectation tends to put people off living more sustainably altogether. They give up entirely or think it's unattainable. To make the world greener, we need more people doing lots of little, better things, not a tiny group of ultra-eco people trying to make up for the excesses of everyone else and engaging in eco-martyrdom.

Once you begin your journey of becoming an Eco-citizen, you'll start finding creative solutions for how to live more sustainably. You'll notice the positive changes in your everyday life, health, and mindset. And that's the beautiful thing about being an Eco-citizen: generally, what's good for the planet is good for you, too. Supporting companies that offer sustainable products feels fantastic. Growing your herbs in a vertical garden on your wall at home is like having instant access to a personal French chef. Walking more and driving less is excellent for your health, and reducing your shopping sprees is suitable for both the Earth and your bank account. Becoming an Eco-citizen is not about depriving yourself. It's about enriching your life in ways you haven't even considered yet – and I can promise you you'll make lots of exciting discoveries along the way.

We have just started to understand the full scale of the damage we are causing to the environment. The rise in popularity of sustainable products and travel shows an awareness building. That's the first step in becoming an Eco-citizen: being aware, being informed, and making choices that count.

2

THE EASY STUFF

'The best choices are the ones that have more pros
than cons, not those that do not have cons at all.'
Ray Dalio.

I'm a teacher by trade, and like any good teacher, I'm obsessed with the three Rs. No, not the basic skills of reading, writing, and arithmetic but the three Rs of an Eco-citizen. Reduce, Reuse, and Recycle - in that order.

Whether someone finds themselves in my math class, tutor group, or guitar ensemble, they will get a lesson in the three Rs. And frankly, I think this lesson is more important than any geometry, algebra, or musical scales that are usually part of my repertoire. Better yet, the three R's are simple, easy to remember, and most importantly, they make an immediate impact.

Reduce

The first step - Reduce - is the most effective. The less you consume, the fewer resources you have to take from the planet and the less pollution you cause. If you're not encouraging new consumer goods production, you're not creating waste. As discussed in the previous chapter, reducing your overall consumption and shopping is the best thing you can do for the environment. Of course, nobody expects you to cut down on everything drastically, but you can start taking small, consistent steps right now:

- Reduce your shopping using the "want" vs. "need" consideration. Buy what you truly need, and see if you can snag a bargain buying second-hand.
- Reduce your consumption of things you'll throw away after a few uses. Some examples include replacing plastic bags with reusable ones, not buying fast fashion items that go out of season every few months, and choosing quality products that will last longer.
- Opt for plastic-free alternatives. Most plastic ends up in the ocean. Even on the most remote beaches in the world, you'll find washed-up plastic on its shores.
- Pick out products with the least amount of packaging and utilize bulk buys whenever you can – some grocery stores, for example, sell produce and other food in bulk bins, and you can bring your own containers for them.

- Choose home appliances that are the most energy-effective using the energy rating provided.
- Reduce water and energy waste – shorten your showers, only use the washing machine when fully loaded, and turn the air conditioning to low speed if you must use it.

Reducing your consumer goods, energy, and water consumption is a big step in the right direction. Altering your diet and moving towards more plant-based foods can also help. The vegan/vegetarian/carnivore debate can get slightly heated, and the expectation that everyone stops eating meat doesn't bode well with reality. But as Eco-citizens, we can appreciate that you (and others) can introduce elements of a plant-based diet and still have your favorite foods, just less often. Currently, it takes seven calories of fossil fuel to produce one calorie of food, so cutting down on highly processed and meat-based meals may be equally suitable for your health and the planet.

As with all the other steps to becoming an Eco-citizen, don't make any radical changes you can't sustain. Instead, adjust gradually: shortening your shower by just one minute saves over 250 pounds of greenhouse gasses per year. If all US households did this, we'd prevent almost 22 billion pounds of GHG annually from being emitted. Unplugging your home computer or laptop while away saves 490 pounds of GHG emitted per year and a few more dollars on your monthly bill. In other words, even small steps add up to more considerable changes, and if you gradually introduce them into your lifestyle, you're more likely to stick with them – or do even better as you go along.

Reuse

The second R – Reuse – is just as important as Reduce. Making the most of what we have is great for our budgets, space (so long, clutter), and the earth. Repairing and reusing old items, be it clothing, an old bicycle, or a piece of furniture, is a fun way to be more eco-friendly. Instead of getting a new wardrobe, give your old one a makeover. That steel bike frame made in 1970 is still good today - the environmental price of digging up the ore, turning it into steel, transporting it, assembling it, painting it, and so on has already been paid. The more that bike gets used instead of being replaced by something new and shiny (and probably not as well-made) is net profit in an environmental sense.

Your grandma's kitchen chairs – perhaps with a lick of paint or new upholstery – will give your home a lot more character than a cheap Ikea set, and you won't be adding to the carbon footprint of making new, low-quality things that will wear and break much faster anyway.

If you're feeling inspired, you can even try a little DIY:

- You can turn an old ladder into a quirky bookshelf.
- Bottle caps can serve as tea lights.
- Old diffuser vessels can store makeup, brushes, or combs.
- Jars for food storage or even cotton buds and q tips.

The list is endless. Reusing old items in creative ways can be fun, and it's something you can do together with your partner or kids – why not take the eco-friendly opportunity and make it into a family arts and crafts session?

Simply maintaining things can also add to their overall reusability. Regularly cleaning, maintaining, and upgrading your laptop will prolong its life. Taking broken appliances to repair shops will get them working again. Refurbishing your iPhone instead of buying a new one will save monetary and environmental costs.

If you know you won't be using something again, share it instead of throwing it out. Donate things to charity shops instead of leaving them in trash bins; if you haven't touched your garage tools in a while, perhaps a neighbor could use them.

A resource shared is a resource doubled: we all know this concept from libraries – why buy 50 books if 50 people can use the same book when timed properly? When shared, 50 people can get the same amount of education, entertainment, inspiration, or joy from one library book.

Most of our things – cars, sports equipment, tools, even clothes – spend most of their lives idly. Why not share them and spread the environmental cost out? People shared tools, horses, and farming equipment back in the day because no one had the money to buy everything. Now, most individuals can afford the monetary price of a car or a golf club set, so we own them ourselves.

But can we afford this in environmental terms?

This is not to say you need to turn Amish suddenly, but things like carpooling and sharing items you rarely use can make a positive contribution. The internet has opened up all sorts of possibilities in this area. If I want a car or a piece of equipment, I rent someone else's. Not only reducing the amount of stuff I buy, but these items are usually of better quality than one I'd buy myself as I'd not be able to justify buying high-quality, high-priced items for one or two uses. Everything from power tools to tents, I can use top-quality items when I need them for much less than buying and, of course, less clutter in my home.

Recycle

Recycling is seemingly a hot buzzword, usually seen as the pinnacle of "green". However, recycling is merely the least harmful way of discarding unwanted things. Recycling doesn't make plastic magically disappear – it just postpones the day when it ends up in the landfill or, worse, in our oceans.

In many ways, recycling might have made us less responsible: we assume that since the plastic bags or packaging is "recyclable", it's OK to use them. It's not: you can only recycle things to a point, after which they'll still end up in the trash. Recycling doesn't give us a free pass to consume as much as we want. It's quite the opposite and should only be the last resort.

Plastic is easily one of the most harmful materials invented in the 20th century. It's cheap and durable, and its uses are so many it's hard to imagine a world without it, but it's slowly killing the planet – and us along with it. Plastic doesn't break down. It only breaks up into smaller pieces. Plastic comes from dead organic matter, and when these pieces are small enough, they start mimicking hormones and playing havoc with the oceanic ecosystem. The production of plastic requires chemicals from fossil fuels, which contributes to global warming; our heavy reliance on plastic prolongs the life of fossil fuel industries.

Plastic is in our oceans, rivers, and soil, harming wildlife and even making its way into the human food chain through microfibers and microplastics consumed by animals. Plastic is now found everywhere, from Antarctica to the Arctic and Mount Everest to the world's deepest seabed, the Marianna Trench. It's choking the life out of seabirds, whales, and turtles, and it doesn't degrade for hundreds of years. Even worse, studies have shown it's now turning up in our bloodstream.

Even when recycled, plastic doesn't disintegrate and doesn't biodegrade, and once it reaches the end of its recycled life, it still winds up in landfill.

Because of this, reducing consumption and freecycling – giving unwanted items away instead of throwing them in the bin – is much more effective than recycling. Wherever you can, reduce or eliminate the use of plastic bags. When grocery shopping, get a reusable water bottle and use a "bag for life" shopping bag. And if you have to get something made of plastic, make sure that it's both recycled and recyclable – in other words, not made from new materials, and you can reuse it at least once more.

It may be unsettling to hear that recycling isn't the 'get out of jail free card' that current thinking led us to believe it was. However, awareness means better choices, and now that you know recycling isn't the answer, you can take steps toward a more sustainable lifestyle using these simple tips:

- Easy swaps: instead of plastic water bottles, use metal ones. Replace all plastic bags with reusable ones that last for life. Avoid buying products with plastic packaging, and use bulk buys whenever possible. Bring a reusable cup when purchasing coffee, ditch plastic straws, and swap plastic phone cases for biodegradable ones (such as bio-polymer).
- Remember your Rs: reduce and reuse first.
- Invent your own Rs: rethink and reconsider your choices, revamp your old items, and repair broken things instead of buying new ones.
- Shift your focus toward experiences rather than things: chances are, a walk in the countryside will do you more good than another Amazon order. Going on a bicycle expedition with your kids will be more beneficial to them than the newest Nintendo. The best things in life, after all, are free.

There are hundreds of other ways to live by the three Rs and apply them to your own life based on your values and circumstances.

3

VOTING GREEN WITH YOUR WALLET

'In a free society, people vote with feet and their wallet.'

Milton Friedman

O ne of the most impactful and accessible steps you can take to become an Eco-citizen is voting green with your wallet. Your shopping has a much more significant influence on the environment than you may think:

- Reducing consumption.
- Buying things that last.
- Purchasing products with Earth in mind.

Becoming a conscious consumer can prevent tonnes of pollution from being emitted into our atmosphere, but it reaches further. Noble Prize-winning economist Milton

Friedman famously said that the two most powerful ways people vote in a free society are with their feet and wallet. When going to the ballot box, we only get two choices every four years, and the results are always questionable. Presidential candidates tend to go back on their promises, and even when they do mean well, the massive bureaucratic machine of the government may often put spanners in the wheels of the best intentions.

However, voting with your wallet directly impacts how we source, produce, ship, and consume products and services. And this isn't just about purchasing things made sustainably: it's also about telling companies what we *don't* want. By buying – or not buying – a product, we give its manufacturer a "yes" or "no" on how they do business. If we purchase, it's a "yes" from us; if it's a quality product with sustainability in mind, it's a great choice.

However, products manufactured using bad practices and companies profiting from perpetuating poverty and environmental destruction, our "no" will cut the demand for their business. Supply will always increase or decrease with demand. If no one buys unsustainable products, it starts making reasonable business sense to change their production methods or even find an alternative altogether. For this reason, our first step is not to demand more of what is good for the environment but to cut the supply of what is not. Nike got lousy press due to the conditions in the 'sweat shops' that supplied them some years ago. What is a lesser known fact is since then, the worker's conditions there have vastly improved. Positive change can happen if companies believe it will affect sales.

We admonish China for all its pollution, but it's easy to

forget that the industries that create this pollution exist to satisfy everyone who voted "yes" for what they produce. If nobody bought the products, there would be no reason for these polluting industries to create them. Sure, words like economy and ecology generally don't go hand in hand (although they should). Still, in a system where money makes the world go round, we must make it unprofitable to be environmentally ignorant.

Whether it's everyday shopping or more extensive purchases like home appliances or a car, you can make a difference by asking a few simple questions:

- Who made this product?
- How far does it have to travel?
- Is it good for the planet?

If you're not happy with the answers, don't buy. It's that simple.

Naturally, not everything is black and white, and it's not always easy to make eco-conscious choices. But even the tiny differences that appear insignificant on the surface can have a snowball effect: for example, buying locally grown tomatoes in season is saying "yes" to local farmers and "no" to large companies that import vegetables from thousands of miles away. The locally grown produce may be a little more expensive, but the price tag of the carbon footprint created by importing goods from halfway around the world is much more significant.

Choosing a washing machine that is more energy-efficient is saying "no" to manufacturers of appliances that consume too much electricity. Buying a product made from recycled materials is saying "no" to products made without sustainability in mind.

Becoming an Eco-citizen means making small but impactful daily decisions, and voting green with your wallet is one of them. It doesn't mean you need to quit your compulsive Amazon Prime or AliExpress habit right now, but you can choose products from companies using more sustainable practices. You will be saying a loud and clear "no" to companies and businesses contributing to destroying the ecology that sustains us.

Simply having that in mind adds awareness, and with attention comes better choices. The next time you shop online or in-store, pause and think about what you're buying. Is this sustainable? Is there a better alternative? Do I even need this? Every choice matters, and by being aware of what you're consuming and how your purchases affect the global economy – and ecology - you're taking a big step to living a more sustainable lifestyle.

The Environmental Price

On the surface, buying things, in essence, is all about the "dollar price". We make consumer choices by getting to an intersection of our budgets, needs, and wants. Usually, budget is the deciding factor, and we all like a bargain.

For an Eco-citizen, however, the dollar price isn't everything. The price tag is just one side of the coin: it tells you a little about what it costs to produce the item, the time and labor that went into it, the tech, and the solution it's offering.

But what is its environmental cost?

The price economics of the market generally doesn't factor in the environmental strain that a product causes (unless it is something that directly affects the price, like an item's scarcity), also known as third-party externalities. These 'externalities' aren't easy to legislate, especially for something as complex as the environment on a global scale, or figure out a dollar cost to compensate for the damage. When there is no financial incentive to behave, companies will likely cut corners to be more profitable. No one has found a way to make companies pay for the environmental cost they cause. Most of us care about the bottom line, and the economic bottom line often means detrimental ecological effects.

Until our leaders figure out a way to make companies pay up and balance out the environmental costs – and this may be a long time coming – it's up to us to do our research and vote green with our everyday purchases. It doesn't mean you need to make grand gestures and buy a brand-new electric car or install solar panels on your roof right now, but it does mean asking yourself questions. Where was the product you're buying made? How was it made, and from what materials? How far has it traveled, and by what method? Is the company that produced it committed to reducing its carbon footprint, making an effort to re-forest the land, or using sustainable resources?

And this is more than just climate change. Even if we put that well-publicized problem aside, many other considerations exist. For instance, one example is that 24 billion tonnes of soil are lost each year due to the production of food and fibers. No topsoil, no growing crops. Who's covering the cost of this loss?

Tyson? Nestle? Nike?

No: the planet is, and it's running extremely low on funds right now.

Buying a trendy new top online or getting that coveted gadget you've been eyeballing may only cost you $50 or $150, but it's costing the Earth a lot more. The global fashion industry emits 1.2 billion tons of CO_2 yearly – more than the shipping and aviation industries combined. The industry's heavy reliance on synthetic fibers (two-thirds of the carbon footprint of a piece of clothing is in its fiber production), its manufacturing practices, and worldwide shipping, among other factors, contribute to the damage. Between 2000 and 2014, the world's clothes output more than doubled – and, no, it's not due to the population growth.

It's due to our shopping.

And you can bet neither designer nor high street brands are paying the price: our habitat is.

The electronics industry may be doing a little better regarding CO_2 emissions. Still, it's far from green: your new flat TV's bright LCD screen used nitrogen trifluoride (NF_3) in its cleaning process, a substance used for polishing silicon chips. Since the emissions of NF_3 aren't measured, nobody can tell precisely how much of this substance enters our atmosphere or just how harmful it is – but we do know NF_3 is both toxic and highly potent, and that can't be good news.

Once again, Samsung or Apple, whose phones need an upgrade every year or two, aren't covering the environmental costs that will linger for hundreds of years.

We are. And as the planet's destruction doesn't adhere

to arbitrary national borders, a more global mindset is needed on this issue.

Becoming an Eco-citizen begins by understanding that not all is what it seems in a world of billions of products. It's on us to do the research and make the right decisions. We can't always make the optimum environmental choice. We sometimes don't have access to the knowledge needed or, worse, have been misled. However, if we do our best, we can make a difference, and each choice adds to the total.

Which companies and products are you voting for with your purchases? It's a simple question, but the positive effects will accumulate if you keep asking it. We are just one person among almost eight billion people; what would the consequence be if we multiply the excellent choices by eight billion? It's up to you to answer this question with the purchases you do and don't make.

Go Green by Going Thrifty

Hearing how much the fashion or tech industries contribute to the climate crisis is shocking. Yet, this isn't to say you can never buy a new pair of jeans or a tablet ever again. That isn't feasible – and remember, a sustainable lifestyle isn't about radical, all-or-nothing choices.

However, you can start making positive changes by simply buying less. Just by reducing your spending, you're already making a green decision. Less spending means less consumption, fewer resources used, less pollution emitted into the atmosphere, and less waste.

Let's face it: we often make impulsive choices regarding shopping. Something catches our eye, and we don't stop to think twice – in a world where anything is just one click away, it's easy to get swept up in mindless buying. Clever marketing messages, ads constantly bombarding us, and social media influencers entice us to buy this item or gadget, and it's no wonder we often give in.

It's by design, not by accident: corporations spend over one trillion dollars annually on marketing, and it's a powerful weapon. Companies wouldn't spend that amount on it if it wasn't profitable. However, you're already stepping out of the enclosed circle by simply being aware of that fact.

The next step is to try and shop mindfully. Before committing to buy something, pause for a second and ask yourself:

- Is this something I truly need, or just something I want?
- If it's something I want, where and how is it produced?
- Is it an impulse want? Should I give in?

You'll be surprised just how much money (and the planet's resources) this one simple trick can save you. It's easy to mistake our wants for our needs in the Western world; after all, we are used to affluence, and as we accumulate wealth, we start seeing our wants as our needs.

But if you look closely, it's not hard to tell whether something you want to buy is a necessity or a mere whim. Will the item help you achieve something, fix something, or do something better? How long do you think you'll use this item? Is it going to be helpful to you for an extended period? Or is it just adding to the clutter?

If you answer honestly, you'll see that you can easily limit your buying – and you'll be surprised just how good it feels.

Our wants and needs are different. At the beginning of your Eco-citizen journey, it won't be easy to let go of some of those wants, and that's OK. Simply being more mindful about what you buy, when, and how can make a difference. Think of it as trying out a healthier lifestyle: you're aware that pizza, chocolate croissants, and pumpkin spice lattes exist, and you're reminded of the fact daily, if not hourly. You probably indulge every once in a while – and that's fine. But you know that if you ate processed foods high in sugar and additives all the time, it would have disastrous effects on your body.

It's the same with shopping: going on an extreme shopping diet cold turkey won't work, but if you're a little more mindful of the overall effects on your wallet and the environment, you may start viewing buying new things a little differently.

And for now, that's all you need to do. The greenest purchase you can make is buying nothing, but it's already a positive contribution even if you reduce your overall shopping.

Another fantastic option is being thrifty and buying second-hand. When you purchase something used, you have already cut the environmental cost in two. No new resources are needed to make this item. You get what you need by buying second-hand, but you're not adding to the excess consumption or eventual landfill. As an avid reader and author, I use a Kindle for the ease of carrying a lot of books in my pocket and being able to re-read edits on the go, but I have never bought one brand new. They are all used, which halves (or more) the environmental cost, as the resources used have been shared between its previous owner and me. The same with all my computers, they are refurbished. So not only cheaper but reducing the environmental cost of my 'lap-topping' wants. They are usually upgraded to have more RAM and hard drive space than the original models.

Thrift stores, swap meets, and 'second-hand September' are trending right now, and for a good reason: it's fun, and it's a good thing to do both for yourself and your family, your wallet, and the planet. You can even look at it as a challenge: how long can you go without buying new clothes, tech gadgets, jewelry, or home appliances? What treasures can you find in thrift stores or online swap sites? It's an exciting experiment to try; if you look at it as a game, you won't feel deprived. Instead, you'll start feeling a lot more creative with your buying choices, and as a side effect, your savings account will start looking much healthier (who said ecology and economics don't mix). Plus, you'll be doing your part.

It's incredible how much wasted stuff is out there; a lot of it is barely used and unwanted. Quirky old furniture, vintage clothing, and used electronic devices still work well – there's no shortage of second-hand items you can find and enjoy. Better yet, instead of adding to the global trash pile, you can swap your unwanted items for something else – that way, you're not throwing usable things away and not spending your hard-earned cash on products made in excess in the first place.

Consuming Better Quality

The adage "buy cheap, buy twice" still rings true. Have you ever wondered why things last a lot shorter than they used to? That's because cheap products generally don't last. They're made to be bought, used a few times, and discarded. Fast fashion, new phones that will need to be upgraded again after a year, household items that wear and break quicker. This all adds to the global overproduction and overconsumption of cheap, poor-quality things that serve little function yet have a high environmental cost. And they have an extra charge for you, too: if you buy something cheap, you'll be repurchasing it soon because the item won't last or won't do its intended job properly.

Everything produced (no matter how 'green') has an environmental price, so the less you consume, the less toll you are exacting on the planet. Still, we live in a modern world, and weaving our clothes and growing our food are too out of reach for most of us. We need to buy clothes, houses, energy, and have a way to get around. And while buying less overall or buying second-hand are both excellent choices to incorporate into your new Eco-citizen lifestyle, sometimes, you can't avoid buying something new.

However, it's also a step towards buying green when you buy quality. Products made with quality last longer: a sustainably produced quality sweater will last longer than three cheap fast-fashion ones.

At first glance, you may feel like buying quality products is just too expensive. But looking at it from a purely mathematical point of view, what's more expensive: a $250 Patagonia jacket that you will wear and enjoy for at least four years to come, or four $80 jackets you'll be replacing every 10 months or so? Being economical is not cheap: it's about getting the most bang for your buck, and you'll get more wear per dollar with higher quality things. The dollar price of a quality item may be higher initially, but it pays for itself in the long run.

In addition, a quality product will have a much smaller impact on the environment as it will last much longer. Instead of wasting resources on three or four low-quality items (usually shipped from thousands of miles away), you'll only buy one, making a dent in the overall consumption scale. A tiny dent, to be sure, but when more and more people embark on a journey to become Eco-citizens, the effects will accumulate.

Buying Green

Once you start looking at things by their environmental cost instead of their dollar cost, you are halfway there. Being an Eco-citizen is a mentality: I see "sustainable" as more of a verb than a noun. It means it's about the overarching philosophy and lifestyle rather than a few compartmentalized decisions.

Looking at it this way, buying green is an obvious choice. Severe financial problems aside, there is no good reason not to purchase sustainable alternatives for your everyday things. And it doesn't just mean organic or local: it's also about efficiency. For example, both hemp and trees are natural, but one acre of hemp produces more paper than four acres of trees. Making things from hemp products isn't just about being 'environmental'. It's also about making more efficient use of land.

The market for green products has increased massively, and there are plenty of great choices out there. Looking for products made using sustainable practices, locally and ethically, is now easier than ever. And it's already working: the rise in Eco-citizens means sustainable products are becoming more profitable. Companies will change their practices if we demand accountability. Even if only to follow the money.

However, what corporations say and do are often two different things. Environmental awareness is increasing, and companies realize they need to offer green solutions. Sadly, many often engage in "greenwashing": on the surface, it appears that the company is making an effort to go green. If you dig deeper, it often transpires that the "green effort" is merely a glitzy marketing campaign.

"Greenwashing" is described as an attempt to make people believe that the company is doing more to protect the environment than it is. In other words, it's conscious consumer misleading, rebranding, repackaging, and remarketing to give the impression of eco-centric products. One example is McDonald's. The company changed the red background of its logo for a green one "to signal its respect for the environment". The restaurant chain has also gotten rid of single-use plastic straws, pledged to have net-zero greenhouse gas emissions by 2050, and claimed to champion animal welfare.

That's all good until you look a little closer and find out that McDonald's still uses the super fast-growing chickens for its meat products. Their zero net GHG emissions by

2050 is an impossible goal, keeping in mind that McDonald's beef footprint alone is responsible for over 22 million tons of greenhouse gases emitted annually. Unless the company drastically alters its menu, all the noble goals and virtuous declarations are empty words.

McDonald's may be the prime example of greenwashing, but it isn't alone. Many corporations are doing their best to appear going green, but it often becomes just another marketing campaign if you dig a little deeper and what businesses don't share typically tells a louder story.

So how do you spot greenwashing? Once again, it's part of the Eco-citizen lifestyle. Being informed is critical, and you can learn to spot fake green promises a mile away. When shopping, look at what the brand is declaring:

- "All our products are made from recycled materials" sounds excellent, but what about the manufacturing process, transport used, and product's carbon footprint? Can they be recycled again?
- "All-natural": is it? If the product claims to be "natural" but has a list of ingredients you can't recognize, it's anything but. Watch out for vague claims: "natural", "eco-friendly", and even "green" are terms that labels can apply very loosely due to insufficient regulation. Your "natural" fruit shake may contain only one grape plus many chemical flavors and additives, and your "green" soap may contain harmful toxins. Always look at the ingredients, not just the label.

- "Pesticide-free", "hypoallergenic", "free-range", and "certified organic" labels aren't always true, either.

It's worth doing some homework and researching the product and the company to make a genuinely informed choice. A good resource for this is Greenerchoices.org, an excellent resource for figuring out labels and choosing green products, not just greenwashed.

Not all of us have the time or the energy to spend hours researching every single product or food item, and it's not always possible to be entirely sure whether the product is green or not. However, as you walk further down the road of becoming an Eco-citizen, you'll be more aware and more informed, and it will help you make better choices every day.

Voting green with your wallet, first and foremost, means that you're shopping consciously and mindfully. Considering whether you need or want something is a big step; making an effort to buy fewer new things and replace purchasing new items with second-hand options is another enormous contribution to being greener. If you aim to buy quality rather than quantity and always keep the dollar price and the environmental cost in mind, your shopping will naturally become more eco-friendly.

Finally, do buy green, but verify – it's easy to fall into the "green trap", so do a little research before purchasing something. And remember, you don't need to be perfect: it's not feasible. However, you can make increasingly better choices by simply being mindful of how you shop, which will have a cumulative effect.

4

HEALTH AND WELLNESS

We all want to be healthy, fit, and feel good. By now, you've probably noticed an interesting pattern: what's good for the planet is good for you, and what's good for you is good for the Earth. Eating more plant-based foods, moving more by walking or cycling rather than flying or driving, and limiting your consumption is excellent news for your health, mind, and environment.

Could the same be said about the health and wellness products we're fond of?

Superfoods or Superfads?

I had a mind-blowing experience in one of Quito's trendy health food stores on a trip to explore the Ecuadorian Amazon. In Europe and North America, we're all familiar with "superfoods" like goji berries, quinoa, chia seeds, açaí , and so on – foods high in nutritional value and considered incredibly important and healthful. Typically, they come from exotic places and cost a lot more than a bag of local blueberries or a handful of hazelnuts.

Well, back in Ecuador, it's the other way around. I vividly recall a sense of disbelief when I spotted a small bag of buckwheat in that health store, marketed as a "superfood" and sold at the equivalent of $8 per bag. Where I come from, the humble buckwheat is just a grain, and you get them at $0.99 per kilo. In Ecuador, it's a highly-priced superfood, but then back home, quinoa is an expensive health miracle, whereas, in Ecuador, it's as commonplace as buckwheat or oats in Europe.

To me, this seemed like the pinnacle of absurdity in our modern food system: instead of eating local, organically-grown, healthful, and nutritious produce, we transport exotic "superfoods" from halfway around the world while our everyday staples like buckwheat are hauled to South America and sold as a trendy – and expensive – breakfast in the upscale part of Quito or Rio de Janeiro.

Don't get me wrong, health and wellness are undoubtedly important. But if you can't live without your açaí smoothies and chia-peppered shakes, think of it this way: is it impossible to find locally-sourced "superfoods"?

The problem with importing exotic foods from faraway places isn't just the environmental cost of transportation and packaging. It goes deeper than that: most of what we now call "superfoods" – quinoa, moringa, avocadoes, cacao – used to be local staples in South and Central America, where local indigenous communities have sustainably grown and eaten these foods for hundreds of years.

Now that big food companies have remarketed and

repackaged these foods to cater to the ever-powerful health and wellness fads and trends. These crops are being grown on a scale – often with catastrophic consequences to local communities. Palm oil is responsible for destructive deforestation in Asia. Still, your quinoa salad lunches directly affect Bolivian farmers because they can't afford their products, much like Colombians can't afford locally grown Colombian organic coffee. As the costs go up due to our demand, the locals are priced out of their food supply because we think açaí will make us leaner and chai more energetic and that there are no local alternatives.

Corporations that produce the "superfoods" aren't doing it super-sustainably, either: in addition to profiting from poverty in places like Bolivia or Guatemala, they're buying up land, devastating local ecosystems with monoculture farming, and adding genetic engineering into the mix.

So what's an Eco-citizen to do? It's simple – do a little bit of research. If you love your superfoods, keep on consuming them by all means. Just look for local alternatives. Goji berries can be replaced by the humble gooseberry that packs an almost identical nutritional value; instead of quinoa, go for the good old oats or buckwheat; leave açaí alone and get yourself some blueberries or cranberries.

When all is said and done, "superfoods" stand for organic, natural, and highly nutritious foods, not just a noun someone has attached to a particular food. You'll quickly find healthful and delicious local substitutes for the most exotic "superfood" options if you can see past the slick marketing campaigns. You'll stay healthy, eat well, and stop contributing to the global exploitation of land, resources, and indigenous communities.

The Story of Bottled Water

Another remarkable example of manufactured demand is bottled water. In the 1960s, no one would ever think of buying water: our parents' and grandparents' generations happily drank tap water and never worried about Evian. When bottled water first appeared in the stores, people found it ridiculous: why would you pay for something you get almost free from your kitchen tap? What are they going to sell us next, bottled air?

Fast forward to today, and we're all obsessed with drinking bottled water. Americans alone consume 600 million gallons of bottled water each year. Globally, this amounts to about a total of 480 billion plastic bottles bought each year – and that results in our oceans, quite literally, swimming in plastic, as about 80% of those water bottles end up in landfill.

But why and how did the shift happen?

In the 1970s, soft drink companies (yes, we're looking at you, Coca-Cola) noticed the demand for soda drinks was dwindling. Marketing sugary drinks can be tricky, and there's only so much Coke you can drink. As health awareness increased, sales began to decline. To save their revenues, the companies started an aggressive marketing campaign trying to give tap water a bad name and making claims that it's not safe, not clean enough, or too chlorinated to drink.

And it worked. Currently, Nestle is making a neat $8 billion revenue from bottled water alone; Danone (Aqua and Bonafont) is raking in $5 billion in bottled water sales, and Coca-Cola is making $4 billion from bottled water each year.

The worst part is that they're telling you bottled water is cleaner and better for you, that it comes from pristine mountain springs or deep natural wells, and that it's tastier than tap water.

Yet, test after test, study after study, has shown that the opposite is true. In the Western world, tap water is often cleaner and safer than bottled water, like in Cleveland vs. Fiji water. Cleveland's tap water was cleaner and tastier than Fiji's when tested. City water often undergoes much more rigorous testing than bottled water and frequently goes so far as to bottle that same tap water and sell it as their own, as was the case with Aquafina and Dasani. It's filtered tap water, bottled up in plastic, and sold for a price.

In other words, drinking bottled water is saying "yes" to the companies profiting from manufactured demand and outright lies and contributing to our planet being trashed with plastic bottles. And if that's still not convincing enough, think of it in purely mathematical terms: around the world, about one billion people don't have access to clean drinking water. Most major cities in the Western world are spending millions on dealing with plastic trash. Call me idealistic but couldn't this money be better used to ensure everyone around the globe can have unlimited access to drinking water as a fundamental human right?

As a conscious Eco-citizen, carry a metal water bottle

with you instead of reaching for a water bottle in the store and refilling it from a tap. You can install a water filter on your tap at home if you prefer to purify it, but drinking tap water in most of North America and Europe is perfectly safe.

Fitness and Weight Loss

You're starting to see repeating patterns and connections when living a greener, more sustainable lifestyle. You're making changes and drawing your conclusions, and when it comes to fitness, you can probably already figure out what's good for you and the Earth.

As with superfood trends, fads tend to take over our fitness regimes. Peloton bikes, Fitbits, hot yoga, home gyms, etc. Staying fit and working out are crucial to our health and our wellbeing. But do you need all that equipment to be active?

Hot yoga may sound holistic and natural, but the amount of energy used per session is astonishing. Gym equipment and kits have increased as never before during the COVID-19 pandemic, and it's not surprising – but the environmental cost of producing all this excess stuff is too much. We can't afford it if we want to keep ourselves in line with the resources our planet can sustainably provide.

Just like natural, organic, locally sourced food is best for your health, being outdoors and moving naturally is one of the best things you can do for your fitness and state of mind. Walking and running outside has no cost and no equipment required, and as a bonus, you'll get your daily dose of sunlight and Vitamin D this way. Cycling and skateboarding, utilizing outdoor gym equipment in the parks, and playing sports outside are good ways to stay in shape. Indoors, there are plenty of bodyweight exercises you can do, join an online yoga class, or watch exercise videos on YouTube – all at a minimal cost and with very little equipment needed. My personal favorite is Sean Vigue, a slightly over-the-top yoga teacher. He produces excellent videos you do with him, suitable for beginners and the more experienced yoga enthusiasts. The benefits of yoga are probably not a topic for this book, but I will anecdotally mention that while I'm the oldest I have ever been, I haven't felt as good physically in at least 10 years.

An influential industry is behind all the magic shakes, supplements, and low-calorie TV dinners when it comes to weight loss. Much like Nestle doesn't exactly have our best interest in mind when selling bottled water, the diet industry doesn't care about your well-being, either: it's all about profit. If you're hoping to lose weight, going plant-based will likely have a much more significant and longer-lasting impact on your health than buying frozen Weight Watchers dinners. You should always consult your physician before making any dietary changes. Still, organic, plant-based foods will benefit you more than any new supplement or heavily processed "zero-sugar" substitute packed with additives, chemical flavorings, and heaps of salt make it palatable.

Health and wellness trends come and go, and it's impossible to keep up with them. But since you're well on your way to becoming an Eco-citizen, you no longer need to. Create your health and wellness routine with the Earth in mind: eat well, move a lot, be outdoors, and be happy.

Simplifying things doesn't mean going basic. It means decluttering your space, mind, and environment from stuff you never needed in the first place. It's about finding your own unique way of being in this world and figuring out what works best for you - and the planet - in the long run.

And let me tell you, it isn't the newest Peloton.

PART 2

THE HOME

5

THE SHOPPING LIST

Having read this far, you may feel you shouldn't buy anything new. However, that's not an option in our world, but your shopping list could look better. Zero consumption and zero waste are not feasible; although people do it, eight billion people aren't going to, but less buying and lower waste are great ways to go.

As with all green choices, the first step is simple: it's about being aware and informed. The more knowledge and experience you accumulate about sustainable living, the easier it will be to make green choices of your own. As you progress on your journey to becoming an Eco-citizen, you will start finding your creative green solutions, digging deeper, and doing more to offset the environmental damage we're all inflicting on our planet.

For now, you can start making a change by following a few simple eco-life hacks listed below. This chapter is about the mindset of a sustainable shopper: by carefully considering what you need instead of giving in to an impulse, you're already doing better. By researching the companies and products you buy, you're more conscious about which brands you support (or don't). You're reducing your carbon footprint by making a few changes in your shopping, energy consumption, and diet.

Efficiency and thrift are the names of the game. Nothing is more green than using the resources you have most efficiently. If you currently don't do a weekly food shop and are more of an eat-on-the-go kind of person (with average working hours increasing, it's easy to understand why), that would be a good start. Buying the ingredients, cooking dinner for the week, and packing lunches for work seems a no-brainer to some, but this is the best place to start when looking at it through an environmental lens. You'll be eating healthier, and your bank balance won't shrink so fast with all those takeaways, overpriced cafes, and quick meals from the small convenience shop—furthermore, no extra waste from takeout boxes (usually plastic).

How far you're willing to take this is up to you: if you want to go raw vegan and aim for zero waste, that's amazing. However, if you adjust your lifestyle little by little – buy less overall and introduce more vegetables into your daily menu – that is already a positive change, too.

Simple eco-life hacks to try right now:

- Replace single-use items with sustainable options. For example, can you buy them in bulk using your containers instead of pre-packaged? Instead of salad bags, why not opt for whole lettuce? You'll be surprised how much you can reduce your waste by going through your fridge and jotting down which items are available without the packaging.

- Grab your reusable water bottle and your reusable shopping bag every time you leave your house. Even when trying to be conscious consumers, we may still make impulse purchases – and it's best to have your reusable bottle or bag with you just in case you need them.
- Bring a packed lunch. At work or running errands, it's often hard to look for sustainable meal options, and we usually buy plastic-wrapped sandwiches or packaged salads to go.
- Choose products that have biodegradable packaging.
- Upcycle glass jars for food and spice containers, and ditch paper towels for reusable cotton ones.
- Be coffee-conscious: French filter coffee is a greener choice than the one packaged in plastic pods.

This is a quick list of small, everyday things you can do better. It won't cost you much in time, energy, or money, but you'll be surprised just how much you'll reduce your waste – and how great it feels!

If you're ready to delve deeper, let's look at several key areas where we can make sustainable changes reasonably quickly and with incredible benefits for the planet, your health, and your wallet.

There's no other way around it for our food: plant-based diets are greener. Many studies conclude, leaving the animal cruelty issue aside, that shifting to a veggie diet could add almost 50% to the global food supply without expanding land used for agriculture. We would use 50% less water, save as much carbon emissions as the entire transport industry, and save those ever-shrinking rainforests from being ruthlessly cut down to make space for crops to feed and house livestock.

The meat industry is one of the worst regarding environmental costs. A whole host of studies will give you conflicting conclusions on how necessary meat is for our diet. Some say having meat (especially red meat) as part of our diet is essential, while others say we would be healthier without it. As in Eco-citizen, you'll have to read the literature and judge yourself based on your nutritional needs. But looking purely through the lens of resource usage, we can see that currently, around the world, to raise cattle, a landmass the size of Africa is needed, and one the size roughly of South America to grow crops, most of which end up feeding animals. Think of it in purely mathematical terms: to produce one pound of beef, between 2,000 and 8,000 gallons of water are used; for one pound of milk's cow, we use almost 2,000 gallons (this includes water for the animal as well as water used for crops and animal feed). While meat is a very efficient form of food from plate to stomach, most of the potential calories are 'wasted' in the animal by growing up and living until slaughter. Those calories and nutrients can be grown straight from crop to plate without the wasteful practice of turning those nutrients into meat form. By contrast, to produce one pound of tofu or unprocessed oats, only 300 gallons of water are used. In addition, a worldwide shift to plant-based diets would reduce greenhouse gasses from food production by a whopping 70%. And while the meat industry is one of the main culprits, seafood isn't much better: overfishing our oceans is causing long-term damage to the deep-sea corals, while bycatch is responsible for wiping out vulnerable species.

Instead of growing crops to feed the animals, why don't we eat the crops? And why not consume more seaweed instead of tuna?

It's a simple idea, but it could make a massive difference for living within the means of our planet.

Now, quitting meat, dairy, fish, and seafood is not an option for many people. Going entirely plant-based at once is not an easy task, and I don't encourage you to try it if you don't feel ready. Going more plant-based should gradually change as with other sustainable lifestyle choices.

Right now, imagining never eating meat again may sound impossible. But could you commit to only eating meat, say, twice a week? Instead of frequent sushi takeout, could you opt for a veggie substitute every once in a while?

The only way to stick with dietary changes is to make them as slowly and painlessly as possible. The first step isn't to take something away but rather to add more good stuff. For example, adding more vegetables to your plate more often will leave you feeling fuller and consuming fewer animal products as a side effect. Gradually increase the size of your salad bowls and your veggie stir-fry dishes, and the size of your steaks and chicken wing meals will shrink automatically. In addition to dairy milk, opt for plant-based milk here and there; once you get used to them, you can replace the dairy for good.

There are plenty of great plant-based alternatives for cheese, cream, and butter – it's just a matter of looking closer and choosing consciously. When planning your weekly grocery shop or meals, see if you can add more vegetables and fruit; once you make a habit, you'll buy less meat and dairy effortlessly.

The great news is that a plant-based diet will leave you feeling healthier, leaner, and happier, too. Plant-based diets are more natural (produce is produced, as opposed to over-processed frozen TV dinners or fast food) and more compatible with our bodies and biochemistry. If we all gradually go plant-based, the positive effect on the environment will be significant. But remember that no one can individually take the weight of the world's problems. It's much better to have more people reduce their meat consumption than one going vegan and setting the bar too high for everyone around them. Looking at the 21 meals (give or take) you have a week, how many could be made plant-based?

Here are a few simple food hacks to increase your vegetable and legume intake and reduce meat, dairy, and fish products:

- Don't attempt to go entirely plant-based immediately. First, add more greens to your meals.
- Next, reduce your overall meat, dairy, and fish intake by replacing these products with delicious veggie alternatives.

- To make the transition easier, remove meat and fish products that are your least favorite. For example, if you don't particularly like tuna salad, opt for a vegetarian option. By eliminating your least-favorite animal products first, you won't feel like you're depriving yourself.
- Introduce more grains and legumes to your diet. Lentils and chickpeas are packed with protein and serve as great meat alternatives for dishes like pasta and curries.
- Look for plant-based meat alternatives such as tofu, tempeh, seitan, and dairy alternatives such as soy or almond milk, nuts, olive oil, and avocado butter.
- Get creative in the kitchen: any vegan meal can be flavourful and delicious when adding herbs and spices.
- If you are craving those BBQ chicken wings or creamy mayo, try to find a vegan alternative first, like cauliflower jackfruit or tofu.
- Next, see if you can slowly shift towards a vegetarian diet. Try to reduce your meat and fish intake to twice a week and see how you feel.

By making these small changes slowly, you're more likely to transition to a plant-based diet and stick with it long-term. In addition to eating less meat, dairy, and fish products, you can also reduce food waste by picking "imperfect" foods at supermarkets or buying from places that sell unwanted "wonky" fruit and veg. Things like think single bananas, ripe avocados, and the like – in other words, foods that are the most likely to end up in the dumpster if no one buys them) and composting your biological waste. Pesticides are not only damaging to the world's ecology. They are detrimental to our health, with significant studies linking them to Parkinson's disease and leaky gut (thinning of the intestinal wall that allows toxins to enter the bloodstream). Because of the many Eco-citizens worldwide, the market has already catered for your needs. There are many places where you can do your weekly shop delivered to your door with organic and ethical produce.

Cosmetics and Makeup: Sustainable Beauty

Whether you're a minimalist regarding your toiletries, cosmetics, and makeup, or someone who enjoys many body care products, you can positively impact your shopping decisions. Mainstream cosmetic products are usually harmful to the environment (and you): they contain toxic chemicals, unsustainably produced palm oil, one of the leading causes of mass deforestation, and microbeads that end up in the stomach of turtles and seabirds. In addition, most cosmetic products' packaging is plastic – and we already know it's a no-go.

However, as consumers demand brands to do better, some indeed do. By doing a little research, you can now switch to cosmetics and beauty brands that are vegan, cruelty-free, and made from sustainably sourced materials. Look for items packaged in biodegradable materials like bamboo fabric, paper, or refillable using multi-use containers.

Body care products made from natural ingredients like essential oils, coconut oils, and other sustainably sourced plant-based components are better for the environment – and your health. Getting rid of products that contain harmful ingredients will make you feel healthier, and you'll be doing your part as a conscious Eco-citizen. It's not impossible to replace plastic body lotion or toothpaste tubes with biodegradable materials: now, sugarcane, bamboo, and wheat derivatives can mimic plastic – except they are biodegradable. You can replace your entire body care and cosmetics with products made with the planet in mind.

Not all beauty brands are making an effort, and those who do may charge a little extra to cover the cost of their well-sourced quality ingredients. However, we've already talked about the dollar price vs. the environmental cost: sure, an ordinary plastic toothbrush is cheaper than a bamboo one. But the plastic toothbrush will end up in the landfill, and you'll probably buy several of them over months. On the other hand, a toothbrush made from sustainable materials will last you much longer – and once its life is over, it will biodegrade.

As with any other product, it's impossible always to make the perfect choices. Sometimes, better options aren't available. However, when you're shopping for body care and beauty products, use these quick hacks to figure out the greenest choices:

- Swap plastic cotton buds, makeup brushes, toothbrushes, and soapboxes for bamboo ones.

- Look for products packaged in bioplastic, biofilm, paper, glass, aluminum tubs, and jars or refillable containers.
- Switch to solid soaps and shampoo: this reduces the packaging, minimizes water waste, and leaves no trace – most solid soaps and shampoo are entirely biodegradable.
- Ditch the wet wipes: Every year, 11 billion wet wipes are used and discarded in the UK alone. Most of them are sewage blockages and floating trash in our rivers. Swap wet wipes for reusable flannel or cotton towels instead.
- If you absolutely must buy something packaged in plastic, see if you can find an option that's both recycled and recyclable.
- Take a close look at the ingredient list: if you see words like parabens, BHA/BHT, parfum, sodium laureth sulfate, and petrolatum, stay away. For a complete list of harmful toxins in beauty products, use this handy resource: https://davidsuzuki.org/queen-of-green/dirty-dozen-cosmetic-chemicals-avoid.
- "Natural" sounding ingredients like palm oil may appear innocent enough, but unsustainably sourced palm oil does an incredible amount of damage to our rainforests. Always check how and where the brand is sourcing its ingredients and whether they're making sustainability efforts.

In addition to buying green beauty products, you can

also embark on a DIY quest. Coffee grounds make for excellent face scrubs, coconut oil is a great natural moisturizer, and a honey and sugar mix makes for a great facial cleanser. Essential oils can be used as a perfume or added to your favorite products. There are no limits to what you can do, and if you're feeling creative, making your body care products from natural ingredients can be fun and extremely rewarding. In addition, you'll save a good chunk of cash this way – and take another step to living a more sustainable lifestyle.

Dress for the Planet's Success

I already touched on the issue of fast fashion, and by now, you know that we can do better than supporting brands that make poor-quality clothing meant to be used a couple of times and thrown away. Unfortunately, the fashion industry is plagued by bad practices: it's not just the environmental strain but its use of third-world sweatshops (yes, it's still happening) and profiting from poverty. There is the argument for having profitable industries that create jobs in developing countries using cheaper labor to compete. But the fairtrade movement has shown that companies can do this without unfairly exploiting workers. There are plenty of options to buy products made in these countries but where the workers get treated and paid fairly. After all, we want industry and jobs in places like Bangladesh but not exploitation. There are plenty of fair trade brands that have clothes made from there.

Every year, the industry burns 132 million tonnes of coal to produce new fibers, and it uses almost nine trillion liters of water for dyeing and bleaching clothes. The numbers aren't pretty, and making your wardrobe greener is an impactful way to reduce your carbon footprint.

If you remember your three Rs, you already know that reusing is the best: instead of buying new clothes, see what you can repair and reuse. Next, head to your neighborhood thrift store instead of the nearest chain retailer: buying clothes second-hand is a fantastic (and fun!) way to renew your outfits. If thrift shops aren't for you, seek out boutique vintage stores: vintage is always in, and you can find incredible statement pieces at no environmental cost.

eBay, car boot sales, Etsy, and online vintage clothing stores are also great places to look for garments that have been pre-owned yet add a bit of oomph to your wardrobe. Better yet, how about swapping clothes with your friends? Be honest – most of your clothes sit in the closet for days, weeks, and months. Why not organize a clothes swap party and invite your friends over? You'll be surprised how enjoyable sharing clothes and revamping your old outfits is. There are now many apps where you can even sell your old clothes. Who said being eco couldn't be profitable?

Here are some more creative ideas on how to minimize your carbon footprint when it comes to clothes and accessories:

- Aim to buy clothes that you can use year-round. It's incredibly tempting to splurge on an entire spring or fall wardrobe, but most clothes will collect dust in your closet for nine or more months of the year.

- Quality over quantity: the fast fashion trend must stop, so buy quality, sustainably made clothing that will last for years instead of repeatedly purchasing low-quality items and adding to the overconsumption and waste. Certain high-street fashion stores sell products that massively degrade after one wash.
- Research the fashion brands. Most mainstream fashion retailers think it's business as usual, but you know better than that – so look for brands that significantly change how they source, produce, package, and transport their products.
- Avoid statement pieces you know you'll only wear once. By all means, accessorize, but make sure you'll use the piece of clothing or jewelry at least 30 times before committing to buy. Alternatively, you can rent a dress or a handbag for a special occasion.
- Look after your clothes and make them last.
- Please don't throw your old clothes away: donate them, give them away, tear them up and use them as washcloths, garage rags, or kitchen towels.
- Repair your clothes. We're so used to the throw-away culture we don't even remember the days when people took their shoes to the cobblers' and their clothes mended by a tailor. You can still do that today! With a little bit of polish and a single resoling, my work shoes went from lasting a year to four: environment cost and economic cost working hand-in-hand.

- If you buy new, buy from sustainable brands.
- Designer or expensive doesn't mean sustainable (or quality). You might assume that the top fashion houses care about sustainability, but the reality is very few of them do. Download the *Good On You* app to check which brands are eco-friendly to be sure.

Breaking up with fast fashion sounds painful on the surface. The convenience it offers is a big part of its success. Still, you'll be much better off once you do: you'll spend less money on clothes while wearing better-quality garments (a high-quality, sustainably made second-hand pair of jeans will last you much longer and look better than several cheap mainstream pairs). You'll have an ethical and green wardrobe, produce less waste, and say a big fat "no" to companies and brands that are depleting our planet's resources and exploiting impoverished regions. If you enlist a few friends on your eco-fashion quest, you'll see how fun it is to browse vintage and thrift stores, swap clothes, and creatively use old clothing instead of throwing it away.

Clean Better

Household cleaning products make up another big part of our spending and consumption. Like body care and makeup, mainstream cleaning products may contain many toxic ingredients. They usually come in plastic containers, which add to landfills after a couple of uses. The good news is that making a positive, green change in your home is one of the most manageable parts.

Simply replacing plastic containers (so long, Tupperware) with glass jars, biofilm, and cardboard boxes is an easy first step. Next up, take a good look at what you're using and how: do you need five different cleaners for your bathroom, kitchen, living room, and so on? Plenty of multipurpose, organic cleaning products are available, and most of them last much longer – and are less harmful to you – than the cheaper mainstream options.

When shopping for soaps, shampoos, and laundry detergents, look for biodegradable products and see if you can find brands that offer refills. You already know cotton towels are better than paper towels, but the same goes for your plastic cling film, aluminum foil, and the like: ditch those and look for sustainable and reusable options instead.

Finally, as with any other product you buy, research and check out the ingredient list. Spending hours on Google checking every item in our fast-paced lives is impractical, but you can use this valuable resource to check just how green your cleaning products are.

https://www.ewg.org/guides/cleaners/

By now, you're well underway to becoming an Eco-citizen, and you already know the basic principles for a sustainable lifestyle. Use them in every area of your life. Household cleaning products need the same amount of consideration and the same three Rs if you want to ensure that what you're buying and using is eco-friendly, or at the very least, less harmful than what you've been using before.

6

HOME AND GARDEN

A shopkeeper once asked me, "Why do you grow your own potatoes? You can get a whole bag for fifty cents."

It's true, and I could get them even cheaper, but he's still thinking solely in economic terms rather than the environmental/health cost.

Growing your food at home is just about the greenest thing you can do: around 40% of food produced ends up in the trash. By growing your food, you're not adding to the waste, nor are you contributing to global warming by buying exotic fruits and vegetables transported in from thousands of miles away. Eating food you have grown is incredibly rewarding and satisfying, and it doesn't matter whether you have a spacious backyard or just a few windowsills.

By growing some of your food, you decide what goes into the soil. By choosing natural, organic fertilizers – or, better yet, homemade compost (turning waste into plant food) - you're not adding to the planet's pollution by hazardous chemicals and pesticides. You also opt not to support the detrimental proliferation of monocultures (corn, soy, and palm oil) that destroy local biodiversity, strip nutrients away from topsoil, and incorporate genetically engineered seeds. We like to think our food is grown and processed with our health and safety in mind, but most of the mass-produced crops are relentlessly sprayed with toxic chemicals, and every year, we lose even more topsoil due to constant tilling. Topsoil is an environmental issue that seems to go under the radar. 95% of food is grown on this uppermost layer of soil, and it has been in decline for years.

Growing your own food benefits your health, wellbeing, and wallet. Remember those super fast-growing chickens McDonald's uses for its burgers and wraps? The same is happening to fruits and veggies, too. You're right on the money if you've ever noticed how differently a garden-grown tomato or strawberry tastes from the ones you get at the supermarket. Home-grown food does taste different, and it has additional nutritional value. Major food companies are doing the same thing the meat industry is doing to animals: maximizing yield and ignoring the loss of quality. A regular, garden-grown tomato naturally yields about 15 to 20 fruit. A genetically engineered, overbred tomato plant produces three times as much – but the result is a less tasteful, watery fruit. A plant cannot support so many fruits and deliver the same amount of nutrients to each one. The fruit and veg you get at the supermarket will often taste bland and have a lesser nutritional value. On average, 38% less nutritious than in the middle of the 20th century. When you grow food, your yield will be smaller, but it will taste much better and deliver a real nutritional punch.

Organic, locally-sourced produce is often more expensive, and growing your own food is a rewarding labor of love that allows you to enjoy fresh fruit, herbs, and veggies for pennies. Seeds and seedlings cost very little, and with clever use of space, you can enjoy an entire mini garden with delicious fresh, seasonal produce every day without spending much.

But what if you don't live in a house with a spacious backyard? All it takes is a little creativity. Patios, decks, and balconies are excellent for potted plants: you can grow fruit, veg, and herbs outside your window. If you live in an apartment with no outdoor space, perhaps you can utilize the rooftop, and if that's not an option, windowsills will do. Vertical gardens are another great idea – all you need is a sheet of net to hang small pots of plants on, or you can make your own DIY vertical garden setup.

As with everything, you don't need to overhaul your living space entirely and create an indoor food forest out of your apartment (although you certainly can). Start with the easy stuff like herbs: spring onions, basil, dill, and sprouts are easy enough to grow even in the smallest of spaces, and you'll see results almost instantly as these plants multiply. Then, add a little fruit like strawberries and dwarf lemons; chili peppers, mini tomatoes, lettuce, and radish will grow well indoors.

All you need is a little garden soil, sunlight, and water. You can grow as much or as little as you want, but it will have a positive effect: you'll reduce your carbon footprint, eat healthier, and enjoy fresher air as plants purify it.

Don't forget to upcycle old containers when planning your home garden instead of buying plant pots. Old buckets, wooden boxes, crates, and other containers can be given a second life as plant pots, and you'll be both reducing your waste and enjoying a completely green, DIY home garden.

Another bonus of having plants in your home is that you'll no longer need air fresheners made from plastic and use energy (think plug-in air fresheners). Instead, plant a few flowers to give your home a pleasant aroma.

If you'd rather have an outdoor garden, see if you could join a community garden: most cities encourage green projects, and if you can't find one, perhaps you can start your own.

Kitchen and Bathroom

We already touched on personal care products earlier, so you know there are plenty of eco-friendly alternatives to your body care. But you can do more to ensure your bathroom is as green as possible. Here are some easy hacks to get you started:

- Refillable containers for shower gel, soap, and shampoo.
- Organic, biodegradable cotton towels are better for your health and the environment than cheap, synthetic ones you'll often be replacing.
- Natural, low-waste mouthwash and biodegradable charcoal or silk floss.
- Long-lasting metal razors instead of single-use plastic ones.
- Ceramic, glass, bamboo, and wooden bathroom accessories.

- Recycled toilet paper – or, if you want to go old school, an attachable bidet.
- Reusable cotton swabs and face towels.
- Zero-waste period products like menstrual cups.

All of these changes aren't huge, and they won't cost you more (in fact, you're likely to save a chunk of change in the long run as you will need to replace items or buy new much less often), but they will make an impact – and, as you already know, every seemingly little effort has a cumulative effect.

Furniture

A couple of generations ago, parents passed furniture down to their kids. You may still have an antique cabinet or a grandfather clock inherited from your grandparents in your home. We don't expect furniture to last long like many things these days.

Most stuff manufactured by modern industries is of poor quality, and we're constantly bombarded to keep consuming, throwing things away, and buying new every year. That's what keeps the economy going – and the planet exhausted.

When it comes to furniture, apply those same three Rs you already know: reduce, reuse, and recycle. First, think honestly: do you need a new coffee table, or are you simply giving in to an impulse?

Next, think about what you can reuse. Repairing old furniture is a great way to minimize your strain on the earth from overproduction and overconsumption. Simply reupholstering a couch will give your living room a makeover – the same as if you'd bought a new sofa. The stuff in your storage, basement, or attic, collecting dust, can probably be repaired: all you need to do is use your imagination and some basic DIY skills.

Swapping furniture with friends or relatives can be fun, and if you need to buy a new bed or a set of patio chairs, first see if you can find them second-hand. You'll be amazed how many treasures lie forgotten in thrift stores and people's garages –you need to look. Finally, if you've decided to buy new, look for furniture made sustainably. Many furniture brands use wood scraps, recycled materials, and resources from responsible forest use.

There's no way around it: your Ikea habit is terrible for the environment (and I know we all treasure things that take that long to build), but you can make green choices right now, spend less, and liven up your home all in one go.

Pets

Is your Jack Russel zero-waste?

It sounds like a weird question, but in reality, pets have a reasonably large carbon foot – or rather, pawprint. Pets eat one-fifth of the world's meat and fish each year, and an area two times the size of the United Kingdom is used to make dry pet food.

In addition, plenty of pet products – from chew toys to pet beds – are far from sustainable. Plastic pet toys are harmful to your dog and the environment; cheap pet beds, cat trees, and bird or hamster cages aren't doing any favors for the planet either. And most pet food brands use nonrecyclable plastic packaging. If you want to go green when it comes to your pet, here's what you can do right now:

- Choose pet beds and toys made from biodegradable or, at the very least, recycled and recyclable materials; better yet, make your own from an old suitcase or crate and old clothes.
- Minimize your pet's accessories: aesthetics is a personal choice, and while your Yorkie's plastic diamante collar looks cute, remember that it will add to the landfill.
- Buy pet food in bulk to avoid using plastic packaging.
- Plant wheatgrass for your hamster, gerbil, or cat for a snack.
- Use compostable poop bags instead of plastic ones when walking your dog.
- Choose pet food free from beef: beef is the biggest offender in the meat industry regarding land and resource use and greenhouse gas emitted.
- Choose pet food made from alternative protein sources such as insects.
- Make a pet kibble from food scraps from your kitchen: chances are, it'll be much healthier for your pet – and better for the environment.

Much like your other choices toward living a more sustainable lifestyle, there is no need for radical decisions. Your German Shepherd isn't likely to turn vegan, and your cat will need to get protein from somewhere. However, like any other family member, you can at least ensure your pet's carbon pawprint reduces – and that goes for getting a pet, too. Ethical issues aside, adopting a pet from a shelter is always an eco-friendlier choice than going to a breeder for a trendy "designer dog". Besides, adopted animals make great companions!

Energy and Heating

Here's an uncomfortable fact: fossil fuels still generate most electricity worldwide.

And it's not just the greenhouse gasses emitted into the atmosphere by burning coal and gas. The oil industry is responsible for most environmental disasters like oil spills, pollution, and releasing toxic chemicals into the environment. The extraction of fossil fuels leads to the deforestation of land and the destruction of ecosystems and generates enormous amounts of waste. Entire swaths of land are used to lay down pipelines and processing facilities. Strip mining is done by blasting topsoil from mountain slopes to expose the underground oil or coal, completely devastating entire ecosystems. Fracking – the process of injecting liquid into underground rock to extract fossil fuel – is destroying the land, poisoning groundwater, and endangering wildlife and indigenous communities. Vast amounts of wastewater are created and discarded recklessly, risking animal and human life.

Despite devastating results, to this day, over 70% of our electricity is still generated from fossil fuels. The good news is that there are already many solutions to the problems with our over-reliance on fossil fuels. As Eco-citizens, it's our jobs to ensure those alternatives become commercially/politically viable. In political greenwashing nuclear power plants have been closing in favor of 'green' energy. Nuclear is much cleaner than fossil fuels (and just as cheap), but the trend over the last few decades is to close them to make way for renewable energy. What happens when renewables can't make up the difference in power generation from the loss of nuclear? Yep, they re-open a coal plant, which is much easier to reconstruct than nuclear. Hardly progressive.

I understand people have reservations about nuclear as it produces waste (and the occasional meltdown). But to put it into perspective, if we took all the nuclear waste that the US has ever produced, it would be 50 feet high in an area the size of a football field, nothing for a country that size. A negative side effect for sure, but much better than the current alternatives.

Reducing your energy use is an essential step to making a difference. The less energy you use, the more we will cut the demand for dirty electricity sources.

Here's what you can do right now to start making a change:

- Unplug your electronics when not in use, especially laptops and computers.
- Use energy-efficient appliances to save electricity.
- Replace energy-wasteful lightbulbs with LED bulbs
- Turn down your refrigerator.

- Maintain your air conditioning and heating systems. Replace filters often, and limit your air-con blasting as often as possible.
- Only do full loads of laundry.
- Air-dry your clothes and dishes.
- Use double-insulated windows to preserve heat.

These changes are small and easy to make, but they will take you one step closer to becoming an Eco-citizen.

Solar Panels

Not everyone has the chance to replace dirty energy with clean wind or solar power. If you live in an apartment or rent a flat, installing solar panels on your roof isn't going to happen. You can choose clean energy sources to power your electronic devices and small appliances. For example, you can hang a small solar panel on your window – it will happily charge your MacBook, speakers, and phone. Another nifty solution is solar blinds – hung outside your windows, they absorb solar energy and can be used to power up your electronics. A solar water boiler is another excellent option, as are solar power banks and windowsill panels. My canal boat has a solar panel. Even though London is not the sunniest part of the world, it provides electricity for most of my electronic items (except heat-producing items like a kettle or hairdryer), and I've never run out of power.

Waste Disposal

I know, I know. You recycle. You separate your plastics and your organics, and that's great – but it's not enough, and you already know that recycling is a last resort rather than something that justifies our reckless use of plastic. Out of a colossal 525,000 tonnes of plastic trays, pots, and tubs alone utilized in households, only 169,145 tonnes are sent for recycling – and even then, after a few cycles, the plastic is most likely going to end up in the landfill. More likely, around 75% of recycling gets rejected at the processing plant and thrown into landfills, lots of that due to having food remains, so ensure you wash your containers before recycling.

Waste disposal is a huge problem, and you can do your part by making these few changes in your waste management:

- Upcycle and freecycle before you throw anything away. So much excellent stuff ends up in the trash, but you can minimize this by giving things away, repairing them, and making something new out of old items.
- Opt for products that are zero-waste and use biodegradable packaging.
- Compost your biowaste compost makes for a fantastic natural fertilizer for your home garden!

7

ECO-MINIMALISM, MINDSET AND EDUCATION

S peaking of decluttering: have you noticed how minimalism and decluttering are making their way into the mainstream? The book-turned documentary "Tidying Up with Marie Kondo" was a giant Netflix hit, and the film "Minimalism" by Joshua Fields Millburn and Ryan Nicodemus started an entire movement. And now, things like budgeting and efficient living have resurfaced as discussion topics.

Why is that?

Is it possible that deep down, we all know buying more and more stuff isn't doing us – or the Earth - any good?

Why do we feel so great when we finally tidy our closets or declutter our homes? Because it's liberating.

The old warning that when you're focused on materialistic goods too much, the stuff you own ends up owning you is still valid. When we're weighed down by clutter, we have less time for things – friends, leisure, sports – and our most treasured possessions aren't things. They're memories, relationships, and experiences. You can price a new smartphone or a pair of shoes, but how do you price an adventure or love?

The question isn't just purely philosophical. People are waking up to the fact that our most valuable asset isn't monetary: it's time. You can always make more money and buy more stuff, but you can't replace the time lost making that money or shopping. There's an excellent exercise to see just how much precious, valuable time you're sacrificing for stuff you likely don't even need in the first place. Let's say you make $20 an hour at your job and want to buy an Apple Watch that costs $530. That monetary cost may not be *that* steep for something you genuinely want.

But are you willing to trade 26 hours of your time for it? More than an entire day of your life you can never get back for a watch? This exercise is not to judge but to make you think from a different perspective. How much of your hours, days, or even weeks are you trading for things, and are they worth it? When functioning correctly, money is an exchange of your time for a smaller amount of time from many other people who brought that product or service into existence.

To add, you already know that every single item produced from new (or even recycled) materials has an environmental cost. That Apple Watch costs $530, or 26 hours of your time, if you're making $20 an hour (more if you include after taxes). But the materials to make the watch were most likely mined in South Africa, possibly by underpaid local miners paying the price with their low wages and potentially hazardous working conditions. The plastic parts come from the oil industry and are manufactured in China, then transported to Mexico, where the whole thing is assembled by underpaid, often minor workers.

Now, the price is ballooning. From South Africa to Mexico, from extraction to manufacturing, the fee is paid by exploiting impoverished people and planetary resources.

Is Apple covering any of those costs? You already know the answer to that. This is where eco-minimalism comes in.

Essentially, eco-minimalism is something you're probably already doing if you've read this far. You've stuck to your three Rs wherever possible, made more conscious shopping decisions, and minimized your impact by buying less. You're wasting less, too, by reusing or giving away old items instead of adding them to the trash. You're saying "no" to fast fashion, overconsumption, and manufactured demand. That's amazing: you are now becoming an Eco-citizen in your own right, and as you progress on your journey, you'll discover more and more ways to live a more sustainable lifestyle.

Eco-minimalism is a part of it. In addition to what you're already doing, you can always keep in mind these simple exercises to make sure you're reducing your carbon footprint every single day and having a positive impact:

- Am I emotionally buying? If so, what triggers it? Identifying your impulses and triggers and examining them objectively will naturally minimize your shopping sprees. 'Influence' by Robert Cialdini is a superb book that helps spot the signs of companies using tactics that compel us to comply and buy. They do this by taking advantage of the fundamental evolutionary behaviors that serve us well in everyday life.

- What am I buying too much of? Could I reduce it?
- Are the things I'm buying adding value or joy to my life?
- Do I enjoy the things I buy for months or years to come?

Having these questions in mind helps you create your narrative and decide what's important to you. Our society is designed in a way to pressure us into buying and doing things we don't necessarily want in the first place, but it's so tempting to give in and keep up with the Joneses (or the Kardashians).

The trouble is that it comes with a high cost to your well-being, bank account, happiness levels, and the environment. Becoming an Eco-citizen means changing that story, refusing to participate in mindless consumerism, and designing your own life on your terms. And while this book is here to give you the means and a little direction, ultimately, it's up to you to make it work - in your way.

For some people, it means going all-in; for others, it may be small, manageable steps over a more extended period. Whichever way you choose, you will be arming yourself with knowledge and understanding along the way, allowing you to see the world and your lifestyle through a different, eco-friendly lens.

The critical thing to remember is that living a sustainable lifestyle isn't about deprivation or martyrdom. At the beginning of this book, you may have felt uncomfortable or deprived when you thought about limiting your shopping without all your current knowledge. You might have thought that you *needed* your takeaway chai latte, new tech gadget, and steak dinners and that your life quality would go down if you stopped enjoying those things.

I hope that by now, you've started viewing it differently. Living a more sustainable lifestyle, first and foremost, benefits you as an individual. We can all agree that being conscious of our spending habits, eating healthier, moving more, and spending more time with our loved ones instead of shopping malls are good things. We all feel that decluttering is liberating, that DIY projects feel better than Amazon Prime, and that making your own choices instead of blindly following fads is a more authentic way to live. It's up to you what you decide to prioritize.

It just so happens that these things are also beneficial for the planet.

Everything is connected in more ways than we can imagine. A healthier, happier, more conscious version of you is better for our planet and the environment. A healthier, more habitable planet is our only way to survive. People always talk about "saving the planet", but it isn't going anywhere. It's survived super-volcanos and asteroids. The more fragile thing is the life that the Earth sustains.

In this light, our appetite for Starbucks, Apple, and Zara suddenly appear irrelevant, and it happens effortlessly. And if you're not quite ready to give it all up just yet, that's OK, too: simply being mindful and consciously considering your choices is already an excellent start.

Sustainability and Kids

If you have children, teaching them about sustainability is extremely important. Your kids' generation will have to face the mess we're leaving them with, and it's best to arm them with knowledge from an early stage.

It doesn't mean you need to suddenly cut their access to the Nintendo games or ask them to stop wearing their favorite Nikes. Children are susceptible to peer pressure, so if you drastically change how they dress and the things they own and send them to kindergarten or school where all the other kids are wearing the newest sneakers or enjoying smartphones, your child will feel like an outcast. Instead, teach them about sustainability little by little, giving them the knowledge and understanding to make different choices independently.

The best way to start is to teach them fun – and green – things to do. If you're designing an indoor herb garden, include your kids in the process and let them plant something of their own. Teach them about waste and composting by showing them how food scraps from your kitchen feed your wheatgrass plants; explain plastic and its effect on the planet. Let your kids label the recycling bins and encourage them to sort their trash. Include your children in your DIY projects, like making pet toys from old clothing or creating plant pots from old boxes or crates. Read books about the Earth with them to stoke their curiosity, and take them on nature hikes and bicycle rides.

Most importantly, teach them by example. Let them see you turning the lights off when you walk out of the room and unplugging appliances when they're not in use. Equip them with reusable water bottles for school, take them on beach walks or forest treks over the weekend – and pick up trash as you go along. Watch kid-friendly documentaries about animals, plants, and our planet to inspire them, and encourage them to take up green projects such as making a plant-based lunch for school together.

It's not always possible to pick out the best school for your child depending on where you live, and often, better education is absurdly expensive. However, you can look for schools that incorporate environmental education in their programs or have volunteering projects, Earth Day activities, or other strategies to teach children about sustainability. Sadly, most of our educational institutions center on the economic aspect of learning, first and foremost, teaching kids to focus on their future jobs, careers, and ways to make money when they graduate. Instead, we should first teach our children to live sustainably since no amount of money will ever make up for the fact that our planet may become unliveable within the next century.

Debt Based Economy

We currently live in a world of hyper-consumerism. The human race's ability to create abundance has led to a problem never seen before, too much of everything. Our attention is constantly diverted by people urging, convincing, and persuading us into consuming more. Any free content we consume usually comes with a price, moments of our attention to be sold to.

With interest rates being artificially reduced since the start of the 21st century, the barrier to entry for people to get into debt and consume even more than their paycheck has been lowered. But the chickens always come home to roost, and it all needs to be paid back...with interest.

A growing economy is essential for job creation and future investments, like pensions, etc. But not all economic growth is created equally. Eco-citizens ask themselves what sorts of things have caused this growth. Where is that economic growth going? Is the consumption that caused the growth in the interest of human flourishing, happiness, and conservation of our habitat?

The sad truth is that a lot of economic growth comes from and goes to one place in the US. The waistlines of its citizens and in the pockets of someone profiting from over-consumption. Many sources say that 2/3's of the US population are obese. People can only buy so much stuff. They only have so much space. However, their stomachs can consume more than needed, and there is always room for dessert.

As Eco-citizens, we aim to live within our means. Having a budget can significantly help with this. That excel spreadsheet staring at you coldly in the face telling you have spent more money on restaurants than you have on rent can be a real eye-opener. While it's not enjoyable, it certainly gets those spending habits under control.

We try not to contribute to the consumerism that puts more strain on the planet than it can handle. Many financial gurus like Robert Kyokosaki would agree that there is good and bad debt. Good debt would constitute an investment, a house, a business, something that will produce returns or accrue in value to compensate for the interest you will have to pay.

But borrowing money merely for consumption is neither good for your material wealth nor the planet. A whole industry is devoted to making sure you spend more money than you have. A typical rate for a credit card is around 30% which means within three years, the interest due would be more than the initial debt. Many people have entered this debt trap. Some manage to use their credit cards, pay the balance off each month, receive the benefits (paid for by the ones who don't), and pay no interest. However, this is not the most common story. If it were, it wouldn't be such a lucrative business.

Currently, there is more debt in the world than actual money. For most, real estate and investments are mainly financed by debt, and governments cover a percentage of their spending with debt. This is what economists mean when they say we are in a debt-based economy.

Economics has been described as the hill on which things like culture, environment, and politics flow. The monetary system we have had for the last 50 years, where the money supply is no longer constrained by being linked to an asset like gold, has created a world of debt, hyper-consumption, and stagnation of wages in real terms.

There are currently no politically possible answers for this. To a lesser or greater extent, all countries survive on this debt-based system. Alternatives such as cryptocurrencies like Bitcoin offer one solution by creating a different economic system that doesn't rely on debt. The rising popularity of cryptocurrencies is partly due to people being aware of this and looking for new ways to store wealth in a way that cannot be inflated away (as money always devalues over time in a debt-based economy). But to become functioning money, you need consensus (voluntary or otherwise), and apart from the government of El Salvador, Bitcoin or any other cryptocurrency does not yet have that consensus. Something to keep an eye on in the future.

PART 3

BEYOND THE HOME

8

WORK, LEISURE AND TRAVEL

Here's a simple fact: feet and bicycle wheels are best, then trains and coaches, motorcycles and cars are less so, and planes are the worst.

It's an uncomfortable truth, but the way we travel and transport ourselves contributes to making the planet less habitable for ourselves. Any internal combustion engine is problematic – its conception, production, and use contribute to global warming, and there's just no way around it. London, where I live, breaks its annual air pollution quota in the first few weeks of the year! This pollution is estimated to take 70,000 years of life expectancy away from the lives of Londoners each year.

However, we're not going back to riding horses any time soon, which had its own environmental consequences with piles of manure covering the streets. Walking everywhere isn't an option if you live in a big city or rural area where everything is spread out.

This is where the sustainable mindset of an Eco-citizen comes into play. To travel more sustainably, whether commuting to work or going on a holiday, you don't need to ditch cars and budget airlines entirely and commit to cycling and walking only. Don't get me wrong, that would be ideal for GHG emissions, but it's simply not realistic for humans. Still, just like with your shopping choices, you can contribute to offsetting your carbon footprint if you make a few slight adjustments to how you get around.

You may have heard that air travel is the most harmful, and it's true for short flights. From a fuel efficiency perspective, planes use less fuel than cars per traveler: a 4,000-mile flight uses 50 gallons of fuel per passenger (assuming that plane is full), whereas a car would need roughly 133 gallons of fuel to cover the same distance. This is because jet fuel is more potent, but there's a caveat: the efficiency of airplanes only comes into play over long-distance. A Boeing burns most of its fuel during take-off, so if you're jetting from London to Barcelona, that flight will use up more resources than a train, coach, or car ride, especially if you're sharing the vehicle. However, for distances over 4,500 miles, car and train rides are more expensive in fuel efficiency.

But like much of the world's problems, it's a little more complicated than that: while planes may be more fuel-efficient, they leave trails of toxic fumes and soot high up in the atmosphere, contributing to global warming. Overall, air travel is responsible for 5% of greenhouse gas emissions.

Again in the interests of onboarding more Eco-citizens, completely cutting out air travel and driving isn't the answer for most of us. We need to get to work, travel for business or leisure, visit friends and families, and switch to only human-powered means of transportation isn't a realistic option for most of us.

However, you can make more intelligent choices regarding how you travel right now. Knowing what you now know about flying, opt to jet-set only when you need to cover large distances. Whenever you can, carpool to reduce your pollution and see if you can commute to work by bicycle or an electric scooter. If you live near your workplace, perhaps you could walk to work – you'll thank those feel-good endorphins released by physical activity, and the planet will thank you for minimizing your impact.

There are more benefits of walking and cycling in an urban environment.

- You can forget about frustrating traffic jams or bus schedule disruption with consistent times for your commute to work.
- Get to work on time. Over short distances in cities, cycling is the fastest way to travel.
- Get a little exercise in while you're at it.
- Save money on transport (my bicycle paid for itself after only three months of saved Metro costs).
- Explore the city you live in and get to the more difficult places using public transport or car.
- Many companies use carbon offsetting. See what options they have to undo their environmental impact.

More and more cities recognize the importance of green transportation, and more bicycle paths and electric scooter rentals are on the menu.

If invented today, I often wonder, would cars be legal?

What's more, most of our vehicles spend their lifespans parked. I'm not telling you to sell your car right this minute or get a Tesla, but you can minimize the harmful effects by walking and cycling more, sharing your car with others, and making do with the vehicle you have now instead of upgrading every five years.

Remember the environmental cost of brand-new things? Second-hand cars have already paid that environmental cost. So if having a personal vehicle is an absolute must for you, see if you can buy one second-hand or, at the very least, resist the temptation to buy a new one every few years. It could also be as simple as moving closer to work or working closer to home (or remotely, as many have experienced working from home in the last few years).

Interrail Your Way Away

Travel isn't just about getting from A to B: if it were, we wouldn't call it 'to travel' in the first place. People increasingly appreciate slow travel and want to enjoy both the journey and the destination. The COVID-19 pandemic was a wake-up call to us all. Most wanderlust-bitten people will tell you they found a new appreciation for travel experiences rather than trendy destinations. With international travel restricted, many people discovered the beauty of local tourism. As a resident of the UK, the highlands of Scotland, the beach coves of Cornwall, and more trips to see friends and family have been some of the most enjoyable travel experiences I have had. The Catskills in upstate New York has seen a massive resurgence as people rediscover the beauty that is close to them.

I find interrailing around Europe or hiking in the Highlands far more satisfying, relaxing, and fun than jetting off for a weekend city break or a 5-star resort in Cancun. Traveling slower and overland makes the journey more enriching than sitting in a cramped, air-conditioned plane.

Everybody is different; for you, air travel may be something you can't live without, at least for now. That's OK, but consider the three Rs when making travel plans. Reduce your overall Airmiles, make the most out of each destination you're flying to, and start looking for more eco-friendly alternatives to travel.

Train rides are incredibly efficient, fast, and comfortable and often come with phenomenal views. In addition, interrailing is budget-friendly, allowing you to travel slower and stop exploring more places. Driving from London to Paris or taking a coach releases much fewer emissions than a flight, and you can take your time getting to know the regions or countries where you're traveling. Plus, by train or coach, you'll get to see the most breathtaking views on your journey.

Finally, travel is all about discovery rather than far away distances, and you'll be amazed at just how much you can discover locally. I'll bet there are some breathtaking places just a few hours' drive from your doorstep, and all it takes is a little research to explore your options. You can also combine travel with fitness: country rambles, mountain hikes, mountain biking, camping, horse riding, and other outdoor activities add flavor to any trip – and most of them are environmentally friendly, as long as you leave no trace.

My mother lives in Portugal, doing some very Eco-citizen activities herself in her retirement. So instead of flying straight from London to Lisbon to visit, I decided to coach it. What a trip that was. It was a little improvised on the way (and some longer coach journeys), but I went from London to Paris, Paris to San Sebastian, San Sebastian to Valldiod, and then had her pick me up at the Portuguese border. Now compare that experience with the stress of the airport, the weight restrictions, and the rigidity of the destination. Taking a coach, I got to see Paris for the first time (and biked around the whole city), had a few lovely days in the beautiful beach town of San Sebastian, and danced with some old-age pensioners in the birthplace of the Spanish language. A slightly more enriching experience than duty-free perfumes and overpriced sandwiches, in my opinion.

Eco-Tourism

In addition to choosing greener means of transport, you can also enrich your sustainable lifestyle by choosing travel itineraries made to be eco-friendly. From volunteering in food forests or permaculture projects in California or Ecuador to staying with the locals and buying food from markets while traveling, eco-tourism is a fantastic way to explore the world.

In essence, eco-tourism is about sustainable travel in more ways than one. When you travel with the environment in mind, you may want to seek out experiences that contribute to nature conservation projects, minimize the negative impacts of tourism on the local social and natural systems, and empower local indigenous communities.

You don't need to shell out thousands of dollars for a

trendy travel agency to design an eco-friendly trip for you. You can do this all by yourself with a little bit of research and creativity.

Here's how to make it happen:

- Choose a destination that's a little off the beaten path. Overcrowding and over-tourism in popular hotspots like Venice, Thai beaches, or Bali are causing severe problems for the locals, so opt for places that aren't overcrowded.
- Look for low-impact means of travel: trains, coaches, or perhaps even a boat ride.
- When booking your accommodation, ignore global hotel chains and opt for locally owned and run guesthouses or homestays. Hotel chains are notorious for greenwashing rather than actual green decisions, so steer clear of the Hilton and stay at a local mom-and-pop instead. Better yet, seek alternative, low-impact accommodations like yurts, community-run eco-hostels, tiny houses, or campsites.
- While traveling, avoid single-use plastics by bringing your reusable water bottle, grocery bag, and cutlery. Be mindful of how much waste you produce and seek recyclable products while on the go. Pack your solid soap and bring the essentials with you – on the go, as tempting and easy as it is to buy things we left at home. You can prevent this with a little bit of planning.
- Aim to eat out at local restaurants using local produce or shop at farmers' markets at your

destination. Yes, McDonald's may sound like a safe and familiar option in Peru or Vietnam, but when you opt for local food, you're reducing your carbon footprint and giving back to the community you're visiting.

- When planning your travel activities, look for low-impact fun: hikes, visiting wildlife sanctuaries, trekking, kayaking, etc.
- If you feel inspired, you can choose to volunteer while abroad – helping out at animal shelters, nature conservation projects, and the like are all great ways to enhance your travel experience.
- If you're traveling long distances, consider programs like Pack for a Purpose: using their website, you can choose by destination or project and bring down supplies that the local communities need. It may be school supplies for kids or pet food, but the point is that you'll be offsetting your carbon footprint and helping out in one move.

Remember that traveling is a great privilege that millions worldwide don't have access to, so use it responsibly. Travel expands our horizons and offers us fresh perspectives. Hopefully, seeing the world with your own eyes will help you realize how we're connected and how every action and choice has a ripple effect. Travel wisely, travel slowly, and give back whenever you can – this way, your journeys will have meaning.

What do you do for fun, and is your fun green?

That may sound like an odd question, but the entertainment industry isn't without fault regarding the climate crisis. Music, film, and TV production has an environmental cost caused by the travel and transportation of actors, producers, and other staff, equipment used, waste generated from props and tech, and energy usage. And while the industry is trying to do better – Warner Bros, for example, recently installed a 600-kilowatt solar roof on their studios, generating 1.15 million kilowatts of renewable energy every year), those glitzy Marvel movies and video games aren't zero-emission.

What about other fun stuff? Whatever hobby or activity you enjoy, take another look at it through a lens of an Eco-citizen. Golf may be great for your health, but the destruction of natural habitats and its love of plastic balls makes golf harmful to the planet. Skiing sounds pretty eco on paper, but ski resorts use a vast amount of precious resources to turn a mountain slope into a human playground. Watching sports on TV may appear innocent enough. Still, considering the carbon footprint of flying teams worldwide and catering to crowds of spectators, Super Bowl isn't exactly environmentally friendly. I've always found playing sports is much more rewarding than watching them.

Any hobby involving human-made equipment, tech gadgets, and energy is likely not green. I know this is upsetting news, but I don't expect people to quit all they do for fun and condemn themselves to a life of lonely countryside walks only (although these are great for your health and mood).

Get creative and think of fun activities and zero emissions simultaneously. Instead of being glued to your phone all the time, whether it's doom scrolling on Instagram or bingeing on Netflix, challenge yourself to read a book or do a DIY project instead. Entertain yourself and your partner or kids by board games, drawing, bike rides, or trips to a local farmers' market. Rent or borrow a bicycle and go on an expedition in a forest nearby, visit art galleries, or attend a local cooking class: you'll be surprised just how much you can do and how it affects your physical and mental well-being.

Don't be tempted to buy gym equipment or a set of weights for fitness. If yoga isn't your thing (and in this author's humble opinion, you are missing out if it's not), there are plenty of excellent exercises where all you need is your body weight. Signing up for a gym membership is greener than buying equipment – remember, a resource shared is a resource doubled. In many urban environments, parks have built-in outdoor gyms where you can get a full-body workout. I've found they have a much more friendly and communal vibe, and best of all, it's free at the point of use (plus, with a portable speaker, you get to decide the music).

For more ideas on how to have a good time without contributing to the global climate crisis, use these simple tips:

- Try gardening – no, you don't need a backyard. You can start a herb garden in your apartment or try growing lemongrass in a pot in your kitchen – it's fun to take care of a plant from seed to table, and as a bonus, you'll always have fresh herbs at hand!

- Quilt: Using old clothing to create something new and beautiful is as environmentally friendly as it gets.

- Get outside: walking, hiking, and cycling are great ways to spend time, get some sunshine and exercise, and let your mind wander. Don't feel like it? Set yourself a goal like running a marathon for a cause – that will give you that extra boost of motivation.

- Take up digital photography. A great way to get to know, capture, and appreciate nature.

- Volunteer: giving feels good, and there are plenty of volunteer projects. Pick up trash in your area, help at a kitchen soup, or contribute to a local animal shelter – every little bit counts.

- Start a blog, a YouTube channel, or a podcast. You can use this book as a starting point: document your journey to becoming an Eco-citizen and share it with others. You never know just how many people you may inspire along the way!

- Learn a language: there's no need to buy courses – nowadays, you can find language apps online and start your journey to fluent French from the comfort of your home.

- Join online communities or eco-campaigns: belonging to a group of like-minded people might just become a new source of motivation for your Eco-citizen journey.

As with all other areas of your sustainable lifestyle, travel and leisure are essential, and trying to cut down on all the air miles and fun at once isn't a good idea. Don't make any sudden moves just yet; instead, try to think outside the box, and don't forget that Eco-citizen lens.

Swapping your car commute for a bicycle ride twice a week is already a positive change. Choosing a mountain trek over an all-inclusive holiday package in some overcrowded tourist hotspot is another. However, there is no one-fits-all formula for sustainable travel and leisure: do what works for you, experiment, and see how far you get. It's OK to make small changes over time, it's OK to make mistakes, and it's OK not to get everything perfect the first time. What matters most is that you're aware and that you're trying. How much and how far you're willing to take this is up to you, but remember that every choice matters, and you matter. Be kind to yourself, but be kind to the planet as well: the two go hand-in-hand most of the time.

9

THE NEXT LEVEL

As Eco-citizens, we vote green with our wallets (and perhaps our feet). And in a society where capitalism is a significant economic driver, this is a guaranteed way to make every vote count. But what of the vote we have every four or five years? It's a real tough one, and in the realm of politics, talking about political parties can be like a religion. Just the words Democratic or Republican (or whatever the noun is in your respective country) can send some people into such a state of irrational hatred that having civil discourse is nigh on impossible. But looking at it through an environmental lens, what have they achieved after all these climate summits and big promises? If you ask the people who protest at all these events (which decay into riots from time to time, frustration perhaps?), their answer is clear, nothing. One seems unwilling ('there is no environmental disaster') and the other unable ('the people who generously donated to my election campaign wouldn't like that'). But we live in a democracy (of sorts), and the right to vote is essential for keeping possible tyrants at bay.

Whether it's a local or national government, support candidates with robust environmental platforms and encourage your representatives to work on biodiversity and wildlife conservation, policies limiting greenhouse gas emissions, and protection of public lands. Of course, do your research to see which candidate will do the most good for the environment and follow policy, not just the brand name of a particular party. Do they have a record of big promises but no delivery? Stay informed, follow many different news sources and opinions, watch documentaries, listen to podcasts and decide which political figures are worthy of your trust (if any).

Joining Communities

Now that you've come this far, it's time to consider the next steps. You may already be living a sustainable lifestyle, but your journey doesn't end here: it's only just beginning, and it's exciting to see where it takes you. If you're starting to feel passionate about sustainable living, joining eco-communities will help you progress. An easy first step is joining an online community, such as the "Sustainable Living" Facebook group: out here, you'll find support and a wealth of tips from other Eco-citizens. From selecting a green wardrobe for a toddler to home DIY projects and alternative living ideas, groups like this can be beneficial if you want to connect with like-minded people, share your journey, and find support. There may be a few 'holier than thou' types in these groups who have sacrificed a lot more doing the things they believe help keep the planet habitable to all animals that occupy it (it's the internet, after all). This sacrifice makes them feel they have the right to criticize people, even those with the best intentions. Don't let that put you off. The friendly, supportive, and helpful people in those groups far outweigh that crowd. Don't get discouraged. The only person you need to compare yourself to is your past self.

Another way to stay in the loop is by joining your local eco-communities and movements.

Projects like Growing Communities (https://growingcommunities.org) help connect urban farmers who grow fruit and veg locally and organically direct to customers, avoiding supermarket intermediaries. You can find similar projects in your area and join in as a customer, farmer, or both: community food growing programs aim to help people live a healthier, greener lifestyle, and it's up to you how – and how much – you want to participate.

If you can't find anything locally, perhaps you can fuel a project of your own: to start with, you can encourage friends and family to try growing some herbs, swap your harvests or sell the surplus to your neighbors. Alternatively, you can reach out to your local municipality to see if any unused land has the chance to be converted into a community garden. While joining an existing community is always easier, starting a green project can feel extremely rewarding. You'll be surprised how quickly people will follow your lead and join in.

Green Activism

Climate activism is another step. This isn't for everyone, and you shouldn't preach the sustainable lifestyle to people who aren't willing to listen – this won't earn you any brownie points, and you may soon start feeling frustrated and alone. Instead, try to show people the positive side of being an Eco-citizen. To change any behavior, you need to focus on the positive rewards rather than guilt or deprivation: people are more likely to listen and join in when you're offering them something beneficial instead of making them feel less-than.

Here are a few helpful pointers to get you started:

- Focus on the good stuff. Instead of criticizing a co-worker for their takeaway coffee habit, tell them how much you're enjoying your sustainable refillable coffee thermos. You could mention how it saves you money and that most brands now offer a small discount if you bring a cup.
- The same goes for the three Rs: don't try to educate people on overconsumption, but rather, tell them how much fun you're having hosting clothes swap parties or making DIY furniture out of old stuff and how much you're saving in the process. If you've saved money by reducing your shopping, reusing old items, and recycling what's no longer needed, perhaps you can now go on that mountain trekking trip you've always dreamed about – share it! Show the positive

results to others to motivate and inspire them rather than guilt-tripping them into making greener choices.

- Pick your battles. Saving the planet is a massive task, and taking on too much may quickly lead to burnout. Instead of trying to do everything, narrow down your focus. What is it you are most passionate? Clean energy? Wildlife and biodiversity conservation? Reduction in plastic? Zero-waste living? Choose what's most important to you and make an effort to support the cause. It could be volunteering, donating money to charities that work in your chosen area, helping get the word out, or supporting activists who are already making a difference. Your contribution matters and every niche area converge into one powerful change stream.

- Educate people by starting a blog, a podcast, a YouTube channel, or a social media account. Simply documenting your journey to becoming an Eco-citizen can be an inspiring platform to motivate and onboard others. You can also focus on just one key area you've selected. It could be creative solutions for biodegradable packaging, water preservation, solar energy, green family living, etc. Whatever you're most passionate about, be outspoken about it and help others find a way to live a more sustainable lifestyle with empathy and understanding.

- Follow and engage with other climate activists on social media. How are they making a change? Can you join them or help them?

Could you help amplify their message?

Climate activism is rewarding work; although it may sometimes feel like you're not making an impact, every effort counts. It already has a cumulative effect if you convince just three people to buy less, shift toward a more plant-based diet, and save energy. If it's an entire neighborhood, you're making a significant change. Imagine what would happen if the message spread like wildfire, and we could all reduce our carbon footprint by half. You can be a part of that wildfire, and the time to act is now. It's also a chance to meet some great people. We have recently lacked social bonds, and meeting people with the same goals as yourself can be revitalizing.

Most importantly, lead by example. If people see you living leaner, cleaner, and greener with a big smile on your face, that will create more Eco-citizens than arguing on Twitter about the pros and cons of animal husbandry.

Self Sufficiency

As I write, energy prices have dramatically increased in my native U.K, as they have around the rest of the world. Factors entirely out of the control of the ordinary citizen have left them at the mercy of extremely high energy costs, throwing some people into poverty and forcing smaller businesses to close.

Unfortunately, this is not the first time that market or political forces have greatly affected the price of these much-needed commodities.

Suppose countries decided to move more towards nuclear, hydro as well as renewables. In that case, it means not only throwing less carbon into the atmosphere, but they would protect their citizens from the price hikes of the most important contributor to human survival, energy. The price of energy affects the price of everything. That fact alone shows how vital to human livability energy is.

On my canal boat, these price increases have affected me much less. My electricity is solar, and I use a wood-burning stove to heat the boat and water. I am not unaffected as I still use gasoline to move the boat around (which I do a small amount every two weeks) and have a gas bottle for cooking, but it certainly softens the blow. The point is not that everyone should live in a canal boat. It's more about having my local power source shields me from these events that are out of my sphere of influence.

Being 100% self-sufficient isn't desirable or practical not only because trade fosters goodwill between countries, allows people to earn a living specializing in what they do best, and helps grow local communities, it's not the most efficient. Trying to recreate by ourselves the thousands of things we use every day is out of the question. "No man is an island," as the saying goes. But having more control over the necessities of life, energy, water, heat, and food and then looking to what your local community can provide is very empowering. It puts you in the driving seat of your personal economy. It can relieve anxiety about events taking place on the world stage without your influence.

I don't grow my food (except a few herbs). I am, however, in contact with my local growing community, where I can get organically grown, fresh fruit and vegetables much cheaper than the supermarket and whose prices are less affected by the increases in energy prices as there are no transportation/packaging costs—a short supply chain from the ground to my plate.

Self-sufficiency can start with something as simple as cooking your own food instead of having someone else do it. It moves on to using the things that are provided in abundance all around us. Taking advantage of the sunshine using solar, where there are plenty of DIY projects like a solar heater, dehydrator, or oven. This can make you more resilient in the areas of energy and heat.

Depending on your property, you can set up a harvesting system to collect the rainwater from your roof. This will ensure you have plenty of extra water during heat waves and be handy for the garden whenever water conservation measures are implemented. For food composing your waste, growing your food, and even having a coop of chickens (as famous farmer Joe Saladin put it, chickens turn scraps into eggs).

How far you go with this, of course, depends on your situation. Still, with the explosion of people vlogging their self-sufficient journeys and giving detailed tutorials on building practical projects at low cost and with simple tools, it's never been easier to take more control over the bare necessities of life.

Alternative Living

Have you ever considered alternative living, like tiny houses, boats, or off-grid living?

This may sound like a far-out idea, but many people

worldwide choose to check out the global consumerist system and live in sync with nature. And, no, it doesn't mean you need to become *Captain Fantastic* and move your family out into the woods living without electricity: it simply means considering different, alternative ways of life.

Tiny houses are the most comfortable transition to living a more sustainable lifestyle. You'll still have all your creature comforts, but you will use significantly less space and energy. If eco-minimalism appeals to you, moving into a tiny house can be a liberating experience. In addition, you can get creative with solar power – for example, covering your roof in solar panels – and become primarily independent from the grid. According to EcoWatch, moving into a tiny house can reduce your carbon footprint from energy consumption by 45%, while your shopping will decrease by 54%. Downsizing in the US could save 366 million acres of biologically productive land if just 10% of people chose tiny houses. Imagine what effect that would have if we were all ready to downsize.

How tiny is a tiny house, though? There's no clear standard, and it's up to you to decide how much space you'll need, but typically, a tiny house is around 400 square feet. You may feel it's too little space, especially if you live in a large home or apartment. However, you'd be amazed just how spacious tiny houses can be with creative interior design solutions. In addition, as you travel further and further down the road to becoming an Eco-citizen, you've probably already become an eco-minimalist, too. Living in a tiny house, just like shopping less or reducing your meat intake, isn't about deprivation: it's about freedom. Imagine being independent of the urban infrastructure, using solar energy, and making your own decisions about growing food, waste management, and use of space.

In addition, building a tiny house isn't about isolation, either. Small house communities are growing and increasingly cropping up around every major city and town worldwide. The city of Den Bosch in the Netherlands, for example, has dedicated an entire piece of land for Minitopia, a community of tiny housebuilders and dwellers. Currently hosting over 30 tiny houses, Minitopia boasts some seriously cool house designs and space for alternative living while still being close to all the city facilities and amenities.

For me, living in a canal boat has been an enriching experience. There is certainly less room, but I don't need much, and it's much easier to manage a smaller space. Living on a boat is much more affordable than renting, let alone buying, a place in London. I'm closer to nature. I focus on experiences more than on things. I feel that living in a boat helps me keep my zen – something I struggled with while living in the hustle and bustle of the city, and nobody turns down an invite to come cruising on the canal.

Abandoning your current house or flat is a radical move, especially if you have a family. However, you don't have to do it right now – it's just something to think about and something to consider for the future, especially if you plan to move in a few years anyway. For now, start with decluttering and downsizing, and if you find the process liberating, perhaps consider the possibility of a tiny house or a boat in the long run. Have a look online, ask to visit a tiny house community, or talk to the boat dwellers: simply connecting with people who live an alternative lifestyle can be the source of motivation and inspiration you need.

Off-grid living is yet another change. Moving to the countryside and building a house with its own energy and water supply is a big step, and it's not for everyone. However, like tiny houses or boats, off-grid living isn't about becoming some oddball hippie outlier with the most basic means. Do a quick search online to see how many unique solutions for off-grid living, including stunning – and comfortable – interiors, spacious gardens, and even food forests right outside your doorstep. Building a house off the grid and installing independent energy and water systems is a big investment upfront. Still, it will pay for itself several times in the long run as you'll have no electricity and utility bills and make your own decisions about land use and growing food. Once again, it's not for everyone – but it's something to consider, especially if you're in the market for a new home.

As mentioned previously, my mother lives out in the sticks in Portugal. To the traditional locals in the village, having clean water supplied from a well or borehole, solar panels, and growing fruits and vegetables (not to mention the homemade red wine) is nothing radical. It just makes sense. Her village is a nice cross-section of all the different levels you can go, from people in colossal modern mansions who live an almost colonial life to the self-sufficient off-the-grid types (I find those people the most fun).

One final step to becoming an Eco-citizen is zero-waste living, although it would be more accurate to say near-zero waste living. Achieving zero-waste is almost impossible unless you hold your breath and eat no food, especially if you live in a city.

Still, the numbers aren't pretty. According to the United Nations Food and Agriculture Organization, we throw away over 7.2 million tonnes of food annually. There are 25 trillion pieces of plastic waste in our oceans; every Christmas and New Year's, we waste an extra five million tonnes of trash in the form of gift wrappers and shopping bags. In one year, we throw 44 million tonnes of newspapers in the US alone; 1,369 tonnes of Styrofoam cups add to the US landfills daily. In the UK, we produce 26 million tonnes of waste annually - 14 million tonnes of which end up in landfills.

The statistics are mind-boggling, and every one of us contributes to trashing our habitat. And while zero-waste living is unattainable for most of us, you can significantly reduce your waste by following these simple steps:

- Do a trash audit. At the end of the week, go through your trash and take notes: could you reduce the plastic packaging you're throwing away? What about other items? Noticing how much you're throwing away can be a wake-up call and let you see where and how you could reduce waste.

- Before throwing anything away, ask yourself: can you repair or reuse it? Could you upcycle the item, or at the very least, utilize it for something else? The less we throw away, the less likely we will keep buying new things.

- Compost your organic waste. Food scraps from the kitchen often end up in the landfill, even when you separate your trash. Why not compost it and use it as fertilizer for your home garden or give it to farmers or community gardens if you don't have one?

- Eliminate single-use items wherever you can. Remember that the production of a new product must pay the environmental cost every time. Switch to reusables as much as possible to avoid adding to the creation and, ultimately, landfill of single-use things.

- Use rechargeable batteries.

- Buy fresh produce instead of packaged salads or fruit.

- Use bulk-buy stores wherever you can, bringing your containers and bags.

- Always aim to recycle.

- Brown-bag your lunch: takeaway food comes with so much throw-away packaging, and you can minimize this by prepping your lunch or, at the very least, bringing utensils.

You can do these things right now, and you'll be amazed just how much you can reduce waste. If you get your friends and family on board, the effect will spread – and as you already know, every effort counts.

Climate activism, alternative living, and aiming for zero-waste may not be for everyone, and that's perfectly understandable. It's OK to do a little here and there than to give up entirely and do nothing. You don't need to follow every step outlined here, but if it at least gives you pause and makes you think differently, you're already on your way to becoming an Eco-citizen.

Useful Resources

Living a sustainable lifestyle is all about making conscious choices, but what those choices will be is entirely up to you. In this book, I've outlined some ways to be greener and eco-friendlier in your everyday life. However, don't stop there: stay curious and informed, do your research, and dig deeper. Below, I list some of my favorite resources to help you stay inspired and motivated to continue your journey as an Eco-citizen.

Earth in Mind, David W.Orr: this is an excellent, mind-set-changing book, written back in 1994, discussing the environmental issues we're facing and fundamental changes we need to make.

Turning the Tide on Plastic, Lucy Siegle: a great book on plastic waste and how to reduce it.

101 Ways to Go Zero-Waste, Kathryn Kellog: a practical blueprint to minimizing your waste – and your carbon footprint.

YouTube Channel by Shelbizleee: a great selection of

YouTube videos to watch, offering practical tips on eco-minimalism.

Game Changers: a documentary film about the benefits of a plant-based diet.

Cowspiracy: a documentary take on modern agriculture and the animal product industry and how it's impacting our planet.

Kiss the Ground: an enlightening documentary on sustainable farming.

Seaspiracy: a documentary focused on overfishing and ocean life.

Breaking Boundaries: The Science of Our Planet: arguably one of the best David Attenborough films on environmental issues – and how we can still fix them.

These are just a few suggestions, and you can continue your research and fact-finding quest by expanding this list and delving deeper. There is plenty of great blogs, podcasts, and video content on sustainable living. I find it's a great technique to refresh your motivation to remain an Eco-citizen by listening to or watching "green" content as part of your weekly routine. It's also a great way to spark discussions with others and stay informed.

AFTERWORD

You matter. Your choices matter. Your voice matters.

I hope this book has made a good case for shifting your mindset toward a more sustainable lifestyle. Not only so that we keep our habitat in good shape for ourselves and future generations, but also by doing so, you will feel the ripple effects on your personal and family life, relationships, and community. To live lean and within boundaries is something nearly all religious texts, philosophies, and self-help gurus advocate for a more fulfilling life. It just so happens it's what is best for the environment. Along the way, you may find you're more and more passionate about eco-friendly choices, and you may join other communities or activist platforms to help spread the message and help others live a more sustainable life. Or, you may find the right balance between no right way to become an Eco-citizen, no clear-cut set of instructions, or a detailed roadmap. You'll have to find your own, and I hope that as you embark on the journey toward sustainability, you'll discover a whole new world of green possibilities that work for you.

The 21st century has forced a whole new mindset on us. For the first time in history, we have reached a point as a species where we know our actions are big enough to affect the entire world's habitation. This idea that the human race's actions make significant changes to the global ecology is relatively new. So it makes sense that all previous centuries have focused on solving problems that create more abundance than working within the constraints of a finite world. It reminds me of the famous 'life finds a way' speech by Jeff Goldblum in Jurassic Park. He talks about how we've spent so much time wondering whether we could do something but never stopped to think whether we should. The 20th century was the ultimate century of 'could we?', 'could we build an atom bomb?', 'could we go to space and further?' 'could we stop the most dangerous diseases?'. It looks like we could. But it certainly wasn't a century of 'should we?', 'should we create things that could annihilate the human race?', 'should we put this chemical in aerosols?', 'should we continue to tear up the planet in a quest for material gain?'. These are the questions for the 21st century.

The previous centuries showed that the human species could do pretty anything we want with the proper funding and goal. This new era should focus on what we should do with this incredible power. Now it's a question of what we should do with that ability. Renewable power, alternatives to plastic, sustainable food production, etc., are already here. We know how to do all these things, but the current economic model doesn't factor in the 'third party externalities' known as the health of the only planet in the universe that provides us with the means to exist. We need to speak for the Earth as she cannot speak for herself. She gives her resources generously and for free. It's up to us to ensure that only the people who solve humans' material problems with Earth in mind get the product of our blood, sweat, and tears.

Finally, I would like to mention that we aren't "saving the planet". The planet will keep revolving around the sun whether or not we are here. It's the delicate natural systems that have been finely (and ruthlessly) tuned over billions of years that we need to worry about, natural systems so complex that even with all our intricate modeling techniques, we don't fully understand. We need to respect those biological systems because we are still ignorant of so much of them (who would have thought 20 years ago that trees use fungi to communicate?). We often don't know how they interlink until they are gone. We need to live in harmony within the systems that allowed the human species to exist, or else in the words of George Carlin, she may "shake us off like a bad case of fleas".

Now that you've started on this path, reuse this book and give it to somebody else – a family member, a co-worker, or a friend. You never know where it may spark a seed of inspiration, and if you've enjoyed it, don't forget to leave a review on Amazon: when it comes to spreading the word, every little helps.

I hope this book helped a little, too.

REFERENCES

Carson, R., & Steingraber, S. (2018). *Rachel Carson: Silent Spring & Other Writings on the Environment* (*LOA* #307) (*Library of America*) (Illustrated ed.). Library of America.

Clear, J. (2022). *Atomic Habits*. Random House Business.

Council, C. (2021, May 31). *Fast fashion needs to slow down for the climate*. Climate Council. Retrieved October 30, 2021, from https://www.climatecouncil.org.au/resources/fast-fashion-climate-change/

Covey, S. R. (2020). *The 7 Habits of Highly Effective People: 30th Anniversary Edition* (4th ed.). Simon & Schuster.

Epstein, A. (2022). *Fossil Future: Why Global Human Flourishing Requires More Oil, Coal, and Natural Gas--Not Less*. Portfolio.

EWG's Guide to Healthy Cleaning. (n.d.). Www.Ewg.Org. Retrieved November 11, 2021, from https://www.ewg.org/guides/cleaners/

Food systems, nutrition and health | *UW School of Public Health*. (n.d.). Washington.Edu. Retrieved December 12, 2021, from https://sph.washington.edu/news-events/news/food-systems-nutrition-and-health

Friedman, M., & Friedman, R. (1990). *Free to Choose: A Personal Statement* (LATER PRINTING. ed.). Mariner Books.

Haidt, J. (2021). *The Happiness Hypothesis: Ten Ways to Find Happiness and Meaning in Life*. Random House Business.

Harari, Y. N. N. (2019). *21 Lessons for the 21st Century* (Reprint ed.). Random House Publishing Group.

Knight, P. (2016, April 26). *Shoe Dog: A Memoir by the Creator of Nike* (First Edition). Scribner.

Kuhn, K., Andersen, K., & Hedges, C. (2016). *Cowspiracy: The Sustainability Secret* (1) (Reprint ed.). Earth Aware Editions.

Kiyosaki, R. T. (2017, April 11). *Rich Dad Poor Dad: What the Rich Teach Their Kids About Money That the Poor and Middle Class Do Not!* (Second). Plata Publishing.

Maloney, M. (2015). *Guide To Investing in Gold & Silver: Protect Your Financial Future*. WealthCycle Press.

Nemiro, K. (2022, January 30). *wellness by kelley*. Wellness by Kelley. Retrieved January 31, 2022, from https://wellnessbykelley.com/blog/2021/8/27/how-to-deal-with-change-boost-productivity

Orr, D. W. (2004). *Earth in Mind: On Education, Environment, and the Human Prospect* (Second Edition, Revised, Second Edition, Revised ed.). Island Press.

PhD, R. C. B. (2021). *Influence, New and Expanded: The Psychology of Persuasion* (Expanded ed.). Harper Business.

Pollan, M. (2022). *The Omnivore's Dilemma: A Natural History of Four Meals by Michael Pollan* (2007–08-28) (Later prt. ed.). Penguin Books.

Sowell, T. (2022). *Basic Economics 4th (forth) edition*. Basic Books.

Thunberg, G. (2019). *No One Is Too Small to Make a Difference*. Penguin Books.

Analysis by Anna Cooban, CNN Business. (2022, August 19). *Why UK energy prices are rising much faster than in Europe*. CNN. Retrieved September 16, 2022, from https://edition.cnn.com/2022/08/19/energy/energy-prices-uk-europe-explainer/index.html

Baraniuk, C. (n.d.). *Why container ships probably won't get bigger*. BBC Future. Retrieved September 15, 2022, from https://www.bbc.com/future/article/20220629-why-container-ships-probably-wont-get-bigger#:%7E:text= There%20are%20around%205%2C500%20container,million%2020ft%20(6m)%20containers.

Goldenberg, S. (2017, July 15). *California drought: authorities struggle to impose water conservation measures.* The Guardian. Retrieved September 23, 2022, from https://www.theguardian.com/environment/2014/mar/11/california-drought-water-conservation

Global Investigation Journalism Network. (2022, May 31). *Tracking Ships at Sea.* Global Investigative Journalism Network. Retrieved September 15, 2022, from https://gijn.org/tracking-ships-at-sea/

Heat in the industrial sector. (n.d.). NRW.Energy4Climate. Retrieved September 15, 2022, from https://www.energy4climate.nrw/en/industry-production/energy-demand-in-the-industrial-sector/heat-in-the-industrial-sector

Leaky Gut Syndrome. (n.d.). Cleveland Clinic. Retrieved September 15, 2022, from https://my.clevelandclinic.org/health/diseases/22724-leaky-gut-syndrome#:%7E:text= Leaky%20gut%20syndrome%20is%20a%20theory%20that%20intestinal%20permeability%20is,letting%20toxins%20into%20your%20bloodstream.

Rakes, M. (2021, October 15). *18 Easy Ways to Become More Self-Sufficient.* Graceful Little Honey Bee. Retrieved September 19, 2022, from https://www.gracefullittlehoneybee.com/18-easy-ways-become-self-sufficient/

Renewable Industrial Process Heat. (2022, September 6). US EPA. Retrieved September 15, 2022, from https://www.epa.gov/rhc/renewable-industrial-process-heat#:%7E:text=According%20to%20a%20study%20of,heat%20above%20750%C2%B0F.

Waddington, E. (2020, April 2). *77 DIY Projects To Improve Your Self-Sufficiency & Keep You Busy*. Rural Sprout. Retrieved September 23, 2022, from https://www.ruralsprout.com/77-diy-projects/

Watts, J. (2021, August 25). *We have 12 years to limit climate change catastrophe, warns UN*. The Guardian. Retrieved November 12, 2021, from https://www.theguardian.com/environment/2018/oct/08/global-warming-must-not-exceed-15c-warns-landmark-un-report